Modern American Remedies

Cases and Materials

Second Edition

1996 Supplement

Douglas Laycock
Alice McKean Young Regents Chair in Law
Associate Dean for Research
The University of Texas at Austin

ASPEN LAW & BUSINESS
Aspen Publishers, Inc.

Library of Congress Catalog Card No. 93-80289
ISBN 0-316-51334-2

Second Edition

Published by Aspen Law & Business
Formerly published by Little, Brown and Company

Printed in the United States of America

Modern American Remedies

1996 Supplement

Contents

Table of Cases

References are to Casebook page numbers; principal cases are in italics.

Table of Statutes, Rules, Constitutions, and Restatements

References are to Casebook page numbers.

Table of Secondary Authorities

References are to Casebook page numbers.

Preface

This supplement includes selected general developments through early 1996, and comprehensive coverage of the Supreme Court's remedies decisions through the end of the Court's Term on July 1, 1996. There are five new principal cases. Two of these replace cases in the main volume, but three, on the measure of injunctive relief, are additions to chapter 3.

United States v. Virginia, on the sexual desegregation of the Virginia Military Institute, and Lewis v. Casey, on structural relief in prison litigation, offer short but significant opinions on remedies issues; they can be read with Hutto v. Finney and the 1990 decision in Missouri v. Jenkins. The 1995 decision in Missouri v. Jenkins, in which the Court finally addressed the scope of the Kansas City desegregation decree, synthesizes issues about the scope of relief, modification of decrees, and the rights of third parties; it inescapably requires an extra day. Throughout these materials, I have interlaced notes on the Prison Litigation Reform Act, a substantial congressional attempt to codify and limit remedies in prison cases.

BMW v. Gore, in chapter 7, can substitute for TXO Production Corp. v. Alliance Resources Corp. Both address the constitutionality of punitive damages; unlike *TXO*, *BMW* has a majority opinion, and for the first time the Court strikes down a punitive damages award on the principal ground of excessiveness. I have written a new note summarizing *TXO*, and the remaining notes to *TXO* should still make sense.

International Union, United Mine Workers v. Bagwell, in chapter 8, replaces the lower court opinion in the same case. *Bagwell* significantly changes previous understandings of coercive contempt and is fairly read to overrule or at least sharply limit part of United Mine Workers v. United States. The changes here are sufficiently substantial that I have rewritten the two sets of notes that accompanied the cases, and Little, Brown has reprinted the revised notes in full instead of directing readers to numerous inserts and deletions.

Douglas Laycock

July 1996

Modern American Remedies

1996 Supplement

CHAPTER 1

Introduction

Page 2. After the first full paragraph, add:

The Court recently reaffirmed that "whether damages are excessive" is a substantive issue controlled by state law in diversity cases. Gasperini v. Center for Humanities, 64 U.S.L.W. 4607 at n.22 (U.S., June 24, 1996); id., Scalia, J., dissenting, at n.12. For the disagreement on how this holding relates to judicial review of federal jury verdicts, see supplement to 188 infra.

CHAPTER 2

Paying for Harm: Compensatory Damages

A. THE BASIC PRINCIPLE: RESTORING PLAINTIFF TO HIS RIGHTFUL POSITION

Page 19. After note 9, add:

There is a long running dispute over competing methods of crediting the settlement against the liability of other defendants. The Supreme Court resolved that dispute for maritime cases controlled by federal law. McDermott, Inc. v. AmClyde, 114 S. Ct. 1461 (1994). The opinion should have persuasive value in other contexts as well.

Liability in federal maritime cases is apportioned on the basis of proportionate fault. In *McDermott*, plaintiff settled with three defendants for $1 million. The jury later found total damages of $2.1 million, apportioned 30 percent to plaintiff and the settling defendants, 32 percent to defendant AmClyde, and 38 percent to defendant River Don. Under the pro tanto rule, the settlement would be subtracted from the verdict; AmClyde and River Don would be jointly and severally liable for $1.1 million. Under the proportionate share rule, the verdict would be reduced by 30 percent, the percentage of fault attributable to plaintiff and the settling defendants. AmClyde and River Don would be jointly and severally liable for 70 percent of $2.1 million, or $1.47 million.

The Court adopted the proportionate share rule, on the ground that it is easier to administer and more consistent with the underlying rule of proportionate fault. The pro tanto rule requires the court to police strategic behavior; if the settling defendants had settled for a dollar, AmClyde and River Don would have been liable for $2,099,999. Either they would have to be permitted to sue the settling defendants for their fair share (a suit for contribution, discussed at 646), or the court would have to review the settlement for reasonableness, or both. These problems do not arise under the proportionate fault rule, because the amount of the settlement is irrelevant to the liability of the nonsettling defendants. They are liable in full for their proportionate share of damages, and the settlement discharges the proportionate share of the settling defendants.

The nonsettling defendants claimed that this violated the one-satisfaction rule, because plaintiff would recover $2.47 million for an injury of $2.1 million. The Court rejected that argument. The excess recovery resulted only because the settling defendants agreed to pay too much. Settlements almost inevitably will be more or less than what a jury would award; if the settling defendants made a bad bargain, that was no concern of the nonsettling defendants.

On the actual facts of *McDermott*, AmClyde escaped liability because of a limitation-of-remedy clause. That complication has been omitted from this explanation.

E. LIMITS ON THE BASIC PRINCIPLE

2. Avoidable Consequences, Offsetting Benefits, and Collateral Sources

Page 108. After note 3, add:

3.1. Suppose plaintiff sues two defendants and settles with one. In most states, the settling defendant's liability will still be submitted to the jury, because it is relevant to the proportionate fault of the other defendant. Suppose the jury finds that the settling defendant was not liable at all, and that the nonsettling defendant was 100 percent responsible. Did the settling defendant just become a collateral source, so that the settlement should reduce damages under statutes repealing the collateral source rule? No, said the court in Kiss v. Jacob, 650 A.2d 336 (N.J. 1994). It would be inconsistent with the comparative fault scheme for the nonsettling defendant to owe less when the injury was entirely his fault than when it was only partially his fault.

Note too that the settling defendant got fresh consideration in the form of a release, that he has no subrogation claim against the codefendant, and that under most proportionate fault schemes, he has no contribution claim against the codefendant.

Page 109. After note 6, add:

6.1. *Helfend* requires that the collateral source be "wholly independent of the tortfeasor," but many states do not follow that rule. A dramatic example that collects the cases is Molzof v. United States, 6 F.3d 461 (7th Cir. 1993). Molzof was permanently disabled due to medical malpractice in a Veterans Administration hospital. His wife left him at the VA hospital, which provided free medical care. But the court, applying Wisconsin law under the Federal Tort Claims Act, awarded $1.3 million for future medical expenses. "Application of the collateral source rule depends less upon the source of the funds than upon the character of the benefits received." Id. at 465, quoting Haughton v. Blackships, Inc., 462 F.2d 788, 790 (5th Cir. 1972).

Molzof was entitled to free medical care because of his service as a veteran, not because the VA had injured him. This entitlement was collateral to his injury, even though the free care came from the very agency that was responsible for defendant's liability. The court also reasoned that Molzof should retain the option to seek medical care elsewhere if at some future time he or his wife became dissatisfied with the VA's care.

Page 110. After note 7, add:

8. The Ohio court has struck down a statute requiring that all compensation from collateral sources be subtracted from the jury verdict before entry of judgment. Sorrell v. Thevenir, 633 N.E.2d 504 (Ohio 1994). The court relied on the right to jury trial, due process, equal protection, and the remedy-for-every-wrong clause of the Ohio Constitution. The reason-

ing is less than clear, but the court clearly thought the statute unfair to plaintiffs.

9. The Kentucky court struck down a similar statute that gave the jurors all the information about collateral sources but didn't tell them what to do with it. O'Bryan v. Hedgespeth, 892 S.W.2d 571 (Ky. 1995). The court relied on a state constitutional provision against limiting recovery for personal injury or wrongful death.

If the legislature cannot agree on the underlying policy dispute over the collateral source rule, does it make any sense to apply the rule to some plaintiffs and not others, at the whim of uninstructed juries? Does it deny equal protection of the laws, because some litigants will be subjected to one rule and other, indistinguishable litigants to a different rule?

3. Proximate Cause and Related Problems

Page 116. After note 5, add:

6. The Court returned to proximate cause in Exxon Co. v. Sofec, Inc., 116 S. Ct. 1818 (1996). The Court held that tort damages in admiralty should be apportioned according to the comparative fault of those whose negligence proximately caused the accident. Where the plaintiff's vessel had maneuvered safely out of the danger created by defendant's negligence, and then due to the captain's gross negligence, the vessel grounded on a reef with resulting total loss while attempting to return to the harbor, the captain's negligence was a superseding cause that broke the chain of proximate causation from defendant's negligence to the accident.

Page 117. After note 5, add:

5.1. Some legislatures have enacted exceptions to the economic harm rule. The Oil Pollution Act, 33 U.S.C. §§2701 et seq. (1994), imposes statutory liability for oil spills in navigable waters. Damages include "loss of profits or impairment of earning capacity due to the injury, destruction or loss of real property, personal property, or natural resources, which shall be recoverable by any claimant." §2702(b)(2)(E). A similar Rhode Island statute applies to any violation of Rhode Island pilotage or water pollution laws. Environmental Injury Compensation Act, R.I. Gen. Laws ch. 46-12.3 et seq. (1991).

The federal act would not apply to *Pruitt* or to any of the cases discussed in notes 1-5, because none of those cases involved oil spills. The Rhode Island act would apply to *Pruitt* and *Testbank*, but not to *People Express* or *General Public Utilities*, because the latter cases did not involve water pollution. Do these distinctions make any sense?

Page 118. After note 8, add:

9. The Illinois court continued to struggle in Congregation of the Passion v. Touche Ross & Co., 636 N.E.2d 503 (Ill. 1994). The court held that the economic loss rule does not apply to accountant malpractice, because an accountant's duty of care, like an attorney's, is defined by law and not by the contract. Thus, victims of accountant malpractice can sue in tort. Two separate opinions thought this should be the rule for all professional malpractice. But the majority was apparently unwilling to overrule a case applying the economic loss rule to architect malpractice. It said the distinction was that attorneys and accountants produce an intangible product, so it is impossible to fully specify the professional's duty in the contract. But the architect's plans will be used to create a tangible building, with characteristics that are "readily ascertainable" and which can be "memorialized in a contract." The separate opinions had great fun with that distinction. Justice Heiple asked how, if the accountant's duty could not be set out in a contract, it was so easily pleaded in a complaint.

Page 125. After the first paragraph of note 6, add:

The Supreme Court of Utah rejected a constitutional challenge to Utah's law excluding seat belt evidence. Ryan v. Gold Cross Services, 903 P.2d 423 (Utah 1995). The court says that exclusion of seat belt evidence is still the majority rule.

5. Substantive Policy Goals

Page 143. After note 3, add:

3.1. The battle over *Sure-Tan* continues. The Seventh Circuit rejected the Ninth Circuit precedents and held that aliens are not eligible for back pay for any period during which they were not legally entitled to be in the country. Del Rey Tortilleria v. National Labor Relations Board, 976 F.2d 1115 (7th Cir. 1992). In 1986, after the incidents at issue in both *Local 512* and *Del Rey*, Congress passed the Immigration Reform and Control Act, which requires employers to verify the citizenship or immigration status of all applicants for employment, and penalizes employers who hire aliens not legally entitled to work. 8 U.S.C. §1324(a) (1994). The Board has since held, in a case arising in the Second Circuit, that workers discharged in violation of the labor laws are entitled to reinstatement conditioned on compliance with IRCA, and to back pay from the date of discharge to the date of reinstatement, or to the date of "their failure after a reasonable time to produce the documents enabling the employer to meet its obligations under IRCA." A.P.R.A. Fuel Oil Buyers Group, 320 NLRB No. 53 (1995). This would seem to have the effect of providing back pay through the whole period of litigation; it remains to be seen whether employers can demand immigration documents at the time of discharge to cut off back pay liability. There were dissents both in the board and in the Seventh Circuit.

3.2. Illegal immigration is not the only source of employment disputes with misconduct on both sides. Consider ABF Freight System v. National Labor Relations Board, 114 S. Ct. 835 (1994). The employer illegally fired the same employee three times; arbitrators or the board ordered him reinstated three times. In the dispute over the third discharge, the employee unambiguously lied to his employer and unambiguously perjured himself before the administrative law judge. Even so, the board found that he had been discharged not for the lie, and not for being late, but because he was on the employer's hit list of union activists. The employer argued that proven perjury should be an absolute bar to any remedy. The Court unanimously held that whether to impose such a rule was up to the board.

3.3. An employee's suit under the employment discrimination laws prompts the employer to more carefully investigate the employee's behavior, and these investigations sometimes reveal resume fraud or on-the-job misconduct such that the employer, if he had known, would have refused to hire the employee or would have discharged the employee for entirely lawful reasons. The Supreme Court recently decided one of these cases, in which a discharged secretary alleging age discrimination had copied her employer's confidential financial records and taken them home. McKennon v. Nashville Banner Publishing Co., 115 S. Ct. 879

(1995). The Court held that the presumptive remedy should be back pay from the time of the unlawful discharge to the time at which the employer discovered the facts that would have resulted in a lawful discharge.

Page 143. After note 4, add:

The Supreme Court has held that no plaintiff can recover damages in federal court "for allegedly unconstitutional conviction or imprisonment, or for other harm caused by actions whose unlawfulness would render a conviction or sentence invalid," unless the conviction or sentence is first reversed or expunged on appeal, on habeas corpus, or by executive clemency. Heck v. Humphrey, 114 S. Ct. 2364, 2372 (1994). So in the hypothetical suit for the consequences of an illegal search, invoking the exclusionary rule to invalidate the conviction would be a prerequisite to any suit for damages.

F. DAMAGES WHERE VALUE CANNOT BE MEASURED IN DOLLARS

1. Personal Injuries and Death

Page 153. After note 2, add:

These kinds of arbitrary distinctions also appear in federal law. For example, loss of society is recoverable under the general maritime law, which applies to seamen killed in territorial waters, but it is not recoverable under the Death on the High Seas Act, 46 U.S.C. app. §761 et seq. (1994). Compare Zicherman v. Korean Air Lines, 116 S. Ct. 629 (1996), with Sea-Land Services v. Gaudet, 414 U.S. 573 (1974). A third set of rules applies to harbor workers, who recover only under a worker's compensation scheme, the Longshore and Harbor Worker's Compensation Act, 33 U.S.C. §901 et seq. (1994).

Page 172. After note 4, add:

For updates on the empirical debate, see Torts: Understanding the Patterns in the Courts, 16 Justice System J. 139 (1993), a special issue with seven articles, mostly suggesting that the tort crisis has been exaggerated, and the studies and criticisms of studies collected in Neil Vidmar and Jeffrey J. Rice, Assessments of Noneconomic Damage Awards in Medical Negligence: A Comparison of Jurors with Legal Professionals, 78 Iowa L. Rev. 883 (1993). Vidmar and Rice criticize the jury-verdict studies on the ground that they fail to take account of which cases go to trial, and more generally, that they fail to take account of the merits of the cases.

Vidmar and Rice experimentally submitted the same medical-malpractice case summary to twenty-one professional arbitrators and eighty-nine individuals who had been summoned for jury duty. Contrary to the conventional wisdom, the median award from the arbitrators was about 20 percent larger than the median award from the jurors, although this difference was not statistically significant. The means differed by less than 2 percent. The juror awards were much more variable, and the largest juror award was 2.4 times the largest arbitrator award. Real jury deliberations would presumably reduce these extremes by forcing jurors to agree on a collective valuation. But the extreme numbers are consistent with the conventional wisdom that the biggest possible verdict in a jury trial exceeds the biggest possible judgment in the same case tried to a judge.

Page 178. After note 6, add:

6.1. For a powerful response to conventional conclusions of the insurance theory of compensation, see Steven P. Croley and Jon D. Hanson, The Nonpecuniary Costs of Accidents: Pain-and-Suffering Damages in Tort Law, 108 Harv. L. Rev. 1785 (1995). Croley and Hanson accept the premise that compensation should track the insurance that consumers would choose to buy for themselves. But they reject the assumption that consumers seek in any simple sense to equalize marginal utility before and after the accident, suggesting that consumers also care in part about equalizing total utilities. They attempt to integrate the two approaches by suggesting that marginal utility curves depend on a total utility baseline. They create an economic model that seems to me much closer to actual human motivations than the marginal utility model.

Croley and Hanson also reject the empirical claim that consumers do not insure against pain and suffering. They argue that uninsured motorist coverage, life insurance on children, accident insurance, double indemnity clauses, and airport flight insurance are all forms of insurance for nonpecuniary losses, and that consumers have not contracted out of pain-and-suffering coverage in contexts where they might have been able to do so. A special case of the second observation is that subrogation clauses in first-party insurance are least common where physical or emotional pain and suffering looms large (life and accident policies), and most common where pain and suffering is insignificant (property and casualty policies).

2. Dignitary and Constitutional Harms

Page 188. After note 1, add:

The Alabama court recently struck down additur as a violation of the state right to jury trial, at least in the context of punitive damages. Bozeman v. Busby, 639 So. 2d 501 (Ala. 1994). The majority reasoned that remittitur protected against deprivations of property without due process, and thus that jury trial and remittitur mediated between two somewhat conflicting constitutional rights, but that plaintiff had no comparable due process right to receive any amount of punitive damages. Could the same reasoning be applied to compensatory damages? Isn't plaintiff's right to compensation a form of property protected by the due process clause?

1.1. The re-examination clause of the seventh amendment provides that "no fact tried by a jury, shall be otherwise re-examined in any Court of the United States, than according to the rules of the common law." This clause applies only to federal courts. The Supreme Court held in the nineteenth century that at common law, only trial judges could set aside a jury verdict as unsupported by the evidence, and that the seventh amendment precluded appellate review of a trial judge's refusal to set aside a verdict. In this century, every federal court of appeals had abandoned this restriction on its power, but the Supreme Court had never passed on the change.

The issue was finally resolved in Gasperini v. Center for Humanities, 64 U.S.L.W. 4607 (U.S., June 24, 1996), in favor of appellate review, but only for abuse of discretion. Justice Scalia, for himself, Thomas, and Rehnquist, filed a rousing dissent based on the plain text of the seventh amendment and the practice of English courts circa 1791; the majority interpreted that practice differently.

All this was collateral to the issue that occasioned the Supreme Court's interest in the case, which was a New York tort reform statute providing for more aggressive review of the amount of verdicts. The federal standard in the Second Circuit is whether the verdict shocks the conscience of the court. In 1986, the New York legislature directed the appellate division to "determine that an award is excessive or inadequate if it deviates materially from what would be reasonable compensation." N.Y. Civ. Prac. L.& R. §5501(c) (1995). The Court recognized that this statute had the substantive purpose of controlling damage awards, but that it acted through the procedural mechanism of changing the relation between judge and jury, and that its application in federal court raised seventh amendment issues.

The majority decided that the federal trial judge could apply the "deviates materially" test as state substantive law in his review of the jury verdict, and that the federal appellate court could review the trial judge's application of the state standard for abuse of discretion, but that the appellate judges could not apply the state standard de novo, as the state law directed. It is not clear whether this is a seventh amendment holding or simply a nonconstitutional holding about federal procedure; presumably, the difference won't matter unless Congress tries to change the result.

Page 190. After note 3, add:

The Supreme Court has adopted the zone-of-danger test for railroad workers' emotional distress claims under the Federal Employers Liability Act, 45 U.S.C. §§51 et seq. (1994). That is, plaintiff must show that defendant's negligence created a zone of physical danger, and that plaintiff was within that zone. Consolidated Rail Corp. v. Gotshall, 114 S. Ct. 2396 (1994). The opinion collects the state cases; the Court acknowledges that the zone-of-danger test is now the rule in only fourteen states.

Three dissenters thought it sufficient that each plaintiffs' emotional distress showed objective physical manifestations. One plaintiff attributed a nervous breakdown to his high stress job as a train dispatcher. The other suffered post-traumatic stress disorder after a friend collapsed in the heat with a fatal heart attack. After plaintiff unsuccessfully administered CPR, his supervisor ordered the crew back to work within sight of the covered body.

3.1. The Prison Litigation Reform Act, 42 U.S.C. §1997e(7)(e) (Supp. II 1996), provides that no prisoner can sue for emotional distress in a federal civil action "for mental or emotional injury suffered while in custody without a prior showing of physical injury."

Page 190. After note 4, add:

For a more recent survey of the cases, see Wilder v. Cody County Chamber of Commerce, 868 P.2d 211, 220-222 (Wyo. 1994). The Wyoming court would permit tort damages only when there is some special relationship between the employer and employee; the most specific examples offered were long service and dismissals to avoid the vesting of retirement benefits.

G. TAXES, TIME, AND THE VALUE OF MONEY

Page 212. After note 6, add:

The Supreme Court in an admiralty case came down strongly on the side of viewing interest as essential to compensation. City of Milwaukee v. Cement Division, National Gypsum Co., 115 S. Ct. 2091 (1995). It rejected the ascertainability rule, and it rejected claims that either a good faith dispute or mutual fault were grounds for reducing or refusing interest. But it said that awards of interest are not automatic; interest can be denied for litigation delay attributable to plaintiff, and perhaps for other unspecified reasons. The case was striking because plaintiff was seeking $5.3 million in interest on a long-delayed $1.7 million judgment.

Page 226. After note 1, add:

For an example of the potential breadth of redeterminations in administrative proceedings, see Metropolitan Stevedore Co. v. Rambo, 115 S. Ct. 2144 (1995). Rambo was an injured longshoreman, receiving compensation under a federal worker's compensation scheme. His disability was permanent and his physical condition did not change. But when he went to crane school and got a better paying job, the employer successfully moved to end compensation for lost wage-earning capacity.

Page 226. After note 3, add:

The Arizona court struck down that state's periodic payment provision, Smith v. Myers, 887 P.2d 541 (Ariz. 1994), under a clause in the state constitution forbidding any law "limiting the amount of damages to be recovered for causing the death or injury of any person." Ariz. Const. art. 2 §31. The court found multiple reasons why periodic payments are less valuable than a lump sum, including the risk that the insurer would become insolvent and an asymmetry in dealing with future events similar to that in the California act. The court also cited an article which argues that lump sums are more valuable because they give plaintiff a choice: A plaintiff who collects a lump sum can buy an annuity, but a plaintiff who gets periodic payments cannot convert them into a lump sum.

CHAPTER 3

Preventing Harm: The Measure of Injunctive Relief

A. PREVENTIVE INJUNCTIONS

Page 234. After note 7, add:

With respect to the new federal rules, Rule 26(a)(1) authorizes local rules to override its provisions. As of March 1994, mandatory disclosure was in effect in only about half the federal judicial districts. Donna Stienstra, Implementation of Disclosure in United States District Courts, With Specific Attention to Courts' Responses to Selected Amendments to Federal Rule of Civil Procedure 26 (Federal Judicial Center 1995).

For a more optimistic view of the tort remedy, see Terry R. Spencer, Do Not Fold Spindle or Mutilate: The Trend Towards Recognition of Spoliation as a Separate Tort, 30 Idaho L. Rev. 37 (1993). The alleged trend is mixed. Spencer claims that nine states and the District of Columbia recognize a tort of intentional destruction of evidence, negligent destruction, or both; he cites ten states as having recently rejected such a tort.

B. REPARATIVE INJUNCTIONS

Page 272. After note 3, add:

4. When the facts are simple and the borders of the violation unambiguous, isn't it obvious that the scope of the injunction must match the scope of the violation? Consider Dalton v. Little Rock Family Planning Services, 116 S. Ct. 1063 (1996), where the lower courts had enjoined enforcement of an Arkansas provision prohibiting the use of public funds to pay for abortion, except to save the mother's life. Overriding federal law required that Medicaid programs also pay for abortions in cases of incest and rape. The Supreme Court unanimously held that the injunction had to be confined to the Medicaid program, and could not extend to all public funds. And because the federal law was embodied in an appropriations rider, which had to be re-enacted each year, and which changed from year to year, the injunction had to be temporally limited to the continued existence of the federal law.

Page 275. After note 9, add:

9.1. For an extremely burdensome prophylactic injunction, treated as routine, see Securities & Exchange Commission v. Posner, 16 F.3d 520 (2d Cir. 1994). The district court enjoined the Posners from acting as directors or officers of any public company, relying on express authorization in the Securities Enforcement Remedies and Penny Stock Reform Act of 1990, 15 U.S.C. §78u(d) (1994). The court of appeals declined to consider whether the act could be applied to violations committed before its enactment; instead, it affirmed on the basis of "'general equitable powers' to fashion appropriate relief." 16 F.3d at 521. The court noted the Posners' long history of culpable violations, and that such remedies had long been routine in SEC consent decrees.

9.2. The Supreme Court reviewed a constitutional challenge to a prophylactic injunction in Madsen v. Women's Health Center, 114 S. Ct. 2516 (1994). The lead plaintiff was an abortion clinic; defendants were pro-life protestors. A state court enjoined defendants from blocking or interfering with public access to the clinic and from physically abusing persons entering or leaving the clinic.

Six months later, the clinic sought further relief. The court found that crowds of protestors in the street and in front of the driveway obstructed access to the clinic despite the earlier injunction. The court granted a new injunction, ordering defendants to stay more than thirty-six feet from the clinic's property line; this had the effect of confining protestors to the other side of the street. The injunction also ordered defendants not to approach, within 300 feet of the clinic, any person entering or leaving the clinic. The Court upheld the thirty-six-foot buffer zone, except as applied to neighboring private property where protest could not obstruct access; it struck down the ban on approaching persons entering or leaving the clinic. It also upheld an injunction against noise audible within the clinic during treatment hours; it struck down a ban on signs visible within the clinic, and a ban on picketing within 300 feet of a residence of clinic employees. Most of the injunction is set out in the Court's opinion.

The applicable remedies law was the law of Florida; the Supreme Court could not consider whether the injunction went further than justified by the violation. But defendants argued that the injunction violated their freedom of speech, and that claim raised analogous issues. The Court held that the appropriate constitutional standard was that the injunction could restrict no more speech than necessary to serve the significant government interests in protecting the rights of the clinic and its patients.

9.3. The Court has agreed to decide a variation on *Madsen*. Pro-Choice Network v. Schenck, 67 F.3d 377 (2d Cir. 1995) (en banc), *cert. granted*, 116 S. Ct. 1260 (1996) The preliminary injunction in *Pro Choice* requires demonstrators to stay fifteen feet away from any person or vehicle seeking access to or leaving from an abortion clinic, except that one or two sidewalk counselors may approach any person in a non-threatening way, but if that person attempts to walk away, the sidewalk counselors must stop counseling and withdraw to a distance of fifteen feet. This is an attempt to serve the purpose of *Madsen*'s ban on approaching persons without wholly preventing communication. The case arose in federal court under state law; presumably the state law of remedies applies, but the court of appeals did not address that issue.

C. STRUCTURAL INJUNCTIONS

1. The Reach of the Injunction When Issued

Page 299. After note 6, add:

The rule that the scope of the remedy must match the scope of the violation received renewed prominence, and cut both ways, in 1996.

UNITED STATES v. VIRGINIA

64 U.S.L.W. 4638 (U.S., June 26, 1996)

[The Virginia Military Institute is a state-supported military college for men only. Severe hazing and lack of privacy are integral parts of the program. The state offers no comparable program for women. The court of appeals held that the male-only program was unconstitutional, 976 F.2d 890 (4th Cir. 1992), but it suggested that Virginia could remedy the violation by integrating VMI, by starting a "parallel" program for women, by privatizing VMI, or perhaps by other means.

The state responded by creating the Virginia Women's Institute for Leadership at Mary Baldwin College. The leaders of VWIL concluded that hazing, lack of privacy, and military drill were pedagogically inappropriate for women; they created a leadership curriculum based on cooperation. The court of appeals affirmed the adequacy of this remedy, subject to continued judicial oversight. 44 F.3d 1229 (4th Cir. 1995).

The Supreme Court affirmed the holding that the men-only program at VMI is unconstitutional. It then turned to the adequacy of the remedy.]

JUSTICE GINSBURG delivered the opinion of the Court. . . .

VI

A

A remedial decree, this Court has said, must closely fit the constitutional violation; it must be shaped to place persons unconstitutionally denied an opportunity or advantage in "the position they would have occupied in the absence of [discrimination]." See Milliken v. Bradley, 433 U.S.

267, 280 (1977). The constitutional violation in this case is the categorical exclusion of women from an extraordinary educational opportunity afforded men. A proper remedy for an unconstitutional exclusion, we have explained, aims to "eliminate [so far as possible] the discriminatory effects of the past" and to "bar like discrimination in the future." Louisiana v. United States, 390 U.S. 145, 154 (1965).

Virginia chose not to eliminate, but to leave untouched, VMI's exclusionary policy. For women only, however, Virginia proposed a separate program, different in kind from VMI and unequal in tangible and intangible facilities. Having violated the Constitution's equal protection requirement, Virginia was obliged to show that its remedial proposal "directly address[ed] and relate[d] to" the violation, see *Milliken*, 433 U.S. at 282, i.e., the equal protection denied to women ready, willing, and able to benefit from educational opportunities of the kind VMI offers. . . . If the VWIL program could not "eliminate the discriminatory effects of the past," could it at least "bar like discrimination in the future"? See *Louisiana*, 380 U.S. at 154. A comparison of the programs said to be "parallel" informs our answer.

[There followed a lengthy showing of VMI's superiority to VWIL in terms of endowment, faculty, student qualifications, athletic facilities, science and engineering curriculum, military training, and alumni network, and of the admitted fact that for better or worse, VWIL does not offer severe hazing and lack of privacy.]

C

When Virginia tendered its VWIL plan, the Fourth Circuit did not inquire whether the proposed remedy, approved by the District Court, placed women denied the VMI advantage in "the position they would have occupied in the absence of [discrimination]." *Milliken*, 433 U.S. at 280. Instead, the Court of Appeals considered whether the State could provide, with fidelity to the equal protection principle, separate and unequal educational programs for men and women. . . .

Valuable as VWIL may prove for students who seek the program offered, Virginia's remedy affords no cure at all for the opportunities and advantages withheld from women who want a VMI education and can make the grade. In sum, Virginia's remedy does not match the constitutional violation . . .

CHIEF JUSTICE REHNQUIST, concurring. . . .

II

The Court defines the constitutional violation in this case as "the categorical exclusion of women from an extraordinary educational opportunity afforded to men." By defining the violation in this way, and by emphasizing that a remedy for a constitutional violation must place the victims of discrimination in the "'position they would have occupied in the absence of [discrimination]," the Court necessarily implies that the only adequate remedy would be the admission of women to the all-male institution. . . . I would not define the violation in this way; it is not the "exclusion of women" that violates the Equal Protection Clause, but the maintenance of an all-men school without providing any—much less a comparable—institution for women.

Accordingly, the remedy should not necessarily require either the admission of women to VMI, or the creation of a VMI clone for women. An adequate remedy in my opinion might be a demonstration by Virginia that its interest in educating men in a single-sex environment is matched by its interest in educating women in a single-sex institution. To demonstrate such, the State does not need to create two institutions with the same number of faculty PhD's, similar SAT scores, or comparable athletic fields. Nor would it necessarily require that the women's institution offer the same curriculum as the men's; one could be strong in computer science, the other could be strong in liberal arts. It would be a sufficient remedy, I think, if the two institutions offered the same quality of education and were of the same overall calibre. . . .

VWIL . . . fails as a remedy, because it is distinctly inferior to the existing men's institution and will continue to be for the foreseeable future. VWIL simply is not, in any sense, the institution that VMI is. In particular, VWIL is a program appended to a private college, not a self-standing institution; and VWIL is substantially underfunded as compared to VMI.

[Justice Scalia dissented on the liability issue; Justice Thomas did not participate.]

LEWIS v. CASEY

64 U.S.L.W. 4587 (U.S., June 24, 1996)

[This was a class action by Arizona prisoners complaining that inadequate law libraries and legal assistance in the state prisons interfered with their right of access to the courts under Bounds v. Smith, 430 U.S. 817 (1977). The Court first clarified (or refined) the substantive right in *Bounds*. "[P]rison law libraries and legal assistance programs are not ends in themselves, but only the means for ensuring 'a reasonably adequate opportunity to present claimed violations of fundamental constitutional rights to the courts,'" quoting *Bounds* at 825. On the majority's conception, a prisoner could not show a violation of *Bounds* unless he showed that he was unable to file some other nonfrivolous complaint, or had some other nonfrivolous complaint dismissed, because of inadequate access to legal information. The district court had made findings with respect to only two such incidents in the whole prison system, both involving inadequate assistance to illiterate prisoners, yet it had entered an injunction regulating the details of law libraries in every prison in the system.

Even assuming that inadequacies in the law libraries would be unconstitutional without proof that these inadequacies actually cut off access to the courts for identifiable complaints, all nine justices appeared to agree that the proven inadequacies in the libraries were scattered and nonsystemic.]

JUSTICE SCALIA delivered the opinion of the Court: . . .

II

A

The requirement that an inmate alleging a violation of *Bounds* must show actual injury derives ultimately from the doctrine of standing, a constitutional principle that prevents courts of law from undertaking tasks assigned to the political branches. It is the role of courts to provide relief to claimants, in individual or class actions, who have suffered, or will imminently suffer, actual harm; it is not the role of courts, but that of the political branches, to shape the institutions of government in such fashion as to comply with the laws and the Constitution. In the context of the present case: It is for the courts to remedy past or imminent official interference with individual inmates' presentation of claims to the courts; it is for the political branches of the State and Federal Governments to manage prisons in such fashion that official interference with the presentation of claims will not occur. Of course the two roles briefly and partially coincide when a court, in granting relief against actual harm that has been suffered, or that will imminently be suffered, by a particular individual or class of individuals, orders the alteration of an institutional organization or procedure that causes the harm. But the distinction between the two roles would be obliterated if, to invoke intervention of the courts, no actual or imminent harm were needed, but merely the status of being subject to a governmental institution that was not organized or managed properly. . . .

C . . .

[W]e turn to the question whether [the two proven] injuries, and the other findings of the District Court, support the injunction ordered in this case. The actual-injury requirement would hardly serve the purpose we have described above — of preventing courts from undertaking tasks assigned to the political branches — if once a plaintiff demonstrated harm from one particular inadequacy in government administration, the court were authorized to remedy all inadequacies in that administration. The remedy must of course be limited to the inadequacy that produced the injury-in-fact that the plaintiff has established. See Missouri v. Jenkins, 115 S. Ct. 2038, 2049 (1995) [reprinted infra at supplement to 344] ("the nature of the . . . remedy is to be determined by the nature and scope of the constitutional violation").

This is no less true with respect to class actions than with respect to other suits. . . .

After the trial in this case, the court found actual injury on the part of only one named plaintiff, Bartholic; and the cause of that injury — the inadequacy which the suit empowered the court to remedy — was failure of the prison to provide the special services that Bartholic would have needed, in light of his illiteracy, to avoid dismissal of his case. At the outset, therefore, we can eliminate from the proper scope of this injunction provisions directed at special services or special facilities required by non-English-speakers, by prisoners in lockdown, and by the inmate population at large. If inadequacies of this character exist, they have not been found to have harmed any plaintiff in this lawsuit, and hence were not the proper object of this District Court's remediation.

As to remediation of the inadequacy that caused Bartholic's injury, a further question remains: Was that inadequacy widespread enough to justify systemwide relief? The only findings supporting the proposition that, in all of [the prison] facilities, an illiterate inmate wishing to file a claim would be unable to receive the assistance necessary to do so were (1) the finding with respect to Bartholic, at the Florence facility, and (2) the finding that Harris, while incarcerated at Perryville, had once been "unable to file [a] legal actio[n]." These two instances were a patently inadequate basis for a conclusion of systemwide violation and imposition of systemwide relief. See Dayton Board of Education v. Brinkman, 433 U.S. 406, 417 (1977) ("instead of tailoring a remedy commensurate with the three specific violations, the Court of Appeals imposed a systemwide remedy going beyond their scope"); id. at 420 ("only if there has been a systemwide impact may there be a systemwide remedy"); Califano v. Yamasaki, 442 U.S. 682, 702 (1979) ("the scope of injunctive relief is dictated by the extent of the violation established, not by the geographical extent of the plaintiff class"). . . .

The constitutional violation has not been shown to be systemwide, and granting a remedy beyond what was necessary to provide relief to Harris and Bartholic was therefore improper. . . .

III

There are further reasons why the order here cannot stand. [First, the district court failed to give sufficient substantive deference to the "legitimate penological interests" asserted by prison authorities, and third, it failed to give those authorities sufficient opportunity to propose their own remedy.]

Second, the injunction imposed by the District Court was inordinately—indeed, wildly—intrusive. There is no need to belabor this point. One need only read the order, to appreciate that it is the *ne plus ultra* of what our opinions have lamented as a court's "in the name of the Constitution, becom[ing] . . . enmeshed in the minutiae of prison operations." Bell v. Wolfish, 441 U.S. 520, 562 (1979). . . .

JUSTICE SOUTER, with whom JUSTICES GINSBURG and BREYER join, concurring. . . .

I . . .

[T]he Court . . . reach[es] out to address a difficult conceptual question that is unnecessary to resolution of this case . . . and divides what would otherwise presumably have been a unanimous Court. . . .

[T]he state of the evidence simply left the District Court without an adequate basis for the exercise of its equitable discretion in issuing an order covering the entire system. . . .

[I]t was an abuse of discretion for the District Court to aggregate discrete, small-bore problems in individual prisons and to treat them as if each prevailed throughout the prison system, for the purpose of justifying a broad remedial order covering virtually every aspect of each prison library.

Other elements of the injunction were simply unsupported by any factual finding. The District Court, for example, made no factual findings about problems prisoners may have encountered with noise in any library, let alone any findings that noise violations interfered with prisoners' access to the courts. Yet it imposed a requirement across the board that the State correct all "structural or acoustical problems." It is this overreaching of the evidentiary record . . . that calls for the judgment to be reversed.

Finally, even with regard to the portions of the injunction based upon much stronger evidence of a *Bounds* violation, I would remand simply because the District Court failed to provide the State with an ample opportunity to participate in the process of fashioning a remedy and because it seems not to have considered the implications . . . for this case [of substantive rules of deference to prison administrators]. . . .

JUSTICE STEVENS, dissenting. . . .

I am persuaded—as respondents' counsel essentially has conceded—that the relief ordered by the District Court was broader than necessary to redress the constitutional violations identified in the District Court's findings. I therefore agree that the case should be remanded. I cannot agree . . . with the Court's decision to use the case as an opportunity to meander through the laws of standing and access to the courts, expanding standing requirements here and limiting rights there, when the most obvious concern in the case is with the simple disjunct between the limited scope of the injuries articulated in the District Court's findings and the remedy it ordered as a result. . . .

[Justice Thomas filed a concurring opinion restating his view that many structural injunctions violate federalism and separation of powers and vastly exceed the proper scope of relief. These views are reprinted in his opinion in Missouri v. Jenkins at supplement to 344.]

NOTES ON THE 1996 DEVELOPMENTS IN THE MEASURE OF INJUNCTIVE RELIEF

1. Early press reports after United States v. Virginia indicated that Virginia authorities thought that they were legally free to privatize VMI, at least in an arms-length transaction in which VMI paid the state for its existing physical plant, but that VMI probably could not raise enough money to survive on that basis. Assuming they found the money, would privatization be an adequate remedy?

2. Is Bailey v. Proctor dead now? Is the Court now unanimously committed to the rightful position principle in injunction cases? That's an unfair question, because there is a 1995 opinion where they split 5-4. See Missouri v. Jenkins, infra at supplement to 344. But the dissents in *Jenkins* at least must be understood in some way that is consistent with the separate opinions in *Lewis*.

3. Should the rightful position principle have equal force in both directions? That is, should the district court have any more discretion to give less than the rightful position in the VMI case than it has to give more than the rightful position in *Lewis*?

4. The Prison Litigation Reform Act is a wide-ranging effort to constrain what Congress regarded as frivolous claims by prisoners and excessive structural remedies by federal judges. Its core provision with respect to structural injunctions is 18 U.S.C. §3626(a)(1)(A):

> Prospective relief in any civil action with respect to prison conditions shall extend no further than necessary to correct the violation of the Federal right of a particular plaintiff or plaintiffs. The court shall not grant or approve any prospective relief unless the court finds that such relief is narrowly drawn, extends no further than necessary to correct the violation of the Federal right, and is the least intrusive means necessary to correct the violation of the Feder-

al right. The court shall give substantial weight to any adverse impact on public safety or the operation of a criminal justice system caused by the relief.

Other provisions of the Act are taken up at appropriate places in this supplement. To briefly summarize in one place, the structural injunction provisions of the Act:

a. forbid relief that "requires or permits any government official to exceed his or her authority under State or local law or that otherwise violates State or local law," unless Federal law authorizes the relief and no other relief will correct the violation of the Federal right. §3626(a)(1)(B).

b. limit preliminary relief to ninety days and to standards analogous to those for the entry of permanent relief. §3626(a)(2).

c. forbid federal courts to order the release of prisoners unless "less intrusive relief has failed to remedy the deprivation of the Federal right" after "a reasonable amount of time to comply," and unless a three-judge court finds by clear and convincing evidence that "crowding is the primary cause of the violation of a Federal right," and that "no other relief will remedy the violation." §3626(a)(3).

d. make all injunctions with respect to prison conditions terminable on motion after two years, unless the court makes new findings that the relief remains necessary on standards analogous to those for entry of initial relief. §3626(b).

e. make all existing injunctions that were entered without the newly required findings immediately terminable on motion unless the court finds that the relief remains necessary on standards analogous to those required henceforth. §3626(b).

f. forbid the entry of consent decrees except on the findings required for litigated relief, but the parties may enter into "a private settlement agreement" that is enforceable only by reinstating the federal claim or by suit for breach of contract in state court. §3626(c).

5. Provisions limiting damage actions and attorneys' fees are codified at 42 U.S.C. §1997 et seq. Provisions attempting to deter or penalize the filing of frivolous claims are codified at 28 U.S.C. §1915 et seq.

6. There were suggestions that the Prison Litigation Reform Act unconstitutionally restricts the remedial discretion of the federal courts. How serious are those objections after *Lewis*? Don't the Court and Congress have pretty similar views of injunctive relief as doing what is necessary to correct the violation, and no more? Assuming that Congress

has eliminated discretionary remedies and left only necessary remedies, compare the holdings in damage cases that Congress can limit compensation for constitutional violations to only certain elements of loss, and need not permit a complete remedy. Schweiker v. Chilicky, 487 U.S. 412 (1988), and Bush v. Lucas, 462 U.S. 367 (1983), described in the main volume at 967. Isn't it a more severe limitation on remedies to eliminate all compensation for some elements of loss caused by a constitutional violation than to limit prospective relief to what is necessary to correct the violation?

7. *Lewis* contemplates that proof of a systemwide violation would justify a systemwide remedy, although the facts did not require definition of a "systemwide violation." Would a "systemwide remedy" be consistent with the Act's directive to remedy only the rights of "a particular plaintiff or plaintiffs"? The Act does not mention class actions, but its provisions for release orders, less intrusive remedies to ease crowding, and deference to "the operation of the criminal justice system" all seem to contemplate that broad relief might sometimes be necessary to remedy the rights of particular plaintiffs.

Page 308. After note 8, add:

9. The Prison Litigation Reform Act addressed these issues with the following cryptic provisions:

> (B) The court shall not order any prospective relief that requires or permits a government official to exceed his or her authority under State or local law or otherwise violates State or local law, unless—
>
> (i) Federal law permits such relief to be ordered in violation of State or local law;
>
> (ii) the relief is necessary to correct the violation of a Federal right; and
>
> (iii) no other relief will correct the violation of the Federal right.
>
> (C) Nothing in this section shall be construed to authorize the courts, in exercising their remedial powers, to order the construction of prisons or the raising of taxes, or to repeal or detract from otherwise applicable imitations on the remedial powers of the courts.

18 U.S.C.§3626(a)(1).

10. Keep in mind that this statute applies only to prison litigation. Does it do anything not already accomplished by the general directive in subsection (A) (quoted supra at supplement to 299) to do only what is

"necessary" to correct the violation of the rights of particular prisoners? *Jenkins II* would seem to satisfy (B)(i) and to be unaffected by (C). Presumably Congress doubted its power to squarely override *Jenkins II*; if federal constitutional and remedial law permits courts to override state tax limitations, and if the use of such power is the only way to remedy violation of a federal right, then the Constitution may require that power to be used. If that reading of the Act is correct, then the real work is done by (B)(ii) and (B)(iii), which specifically apply to this issue the general standard of necessity from subsection (A).

2. Modifying Injunctions

Page 326. After note 10, add:

11. A plurality of the Seventh Circuit en banc has announced a right of government defendants to repudiate consent decrees that appears to go well beyond *Rufo*. Evans v. City of Chicago, 10 F.3d 474 (7th Cir. 1993). The opinion would also limit the power of governments to enter into consent decrees in the first place. "Unless there is a substantial claim under federal law, the district judge should not enter or continue to enforce a consent decree affecting the operation of a governmental body." Id. at 482.

Evans is even more ambiguous than *Rufo* over what was settled and what was litigated. But the five-judge plurality says that the city was not bound by consent, because the consent of one mayor was not binding on future mayors, and that it was not bound by judicial decree, because the court now believes that its earlier decision in favor of plaintiffs was mistaken and that plaintiffs had no substantial claim. Consent without a substantial basis in federal law is insufficient, because it might be a means for elected officials to do things they have no power to do on their own. However, a consent decree is binding if it "compromises genuine uncertainties" about federal law, because in that case the consenting defendant "actually may be enhancing or preserving the powers of the democratic branch (by avoiding a worse outcome after trial) rather than ceding the powers of the government." Id. at 478-479. Five dissenters charged that "the plurality opinion effectively deprives state and local governments of the ability to enter into enforceable consent decrees." Id. at 483 (Cudahy, J., dissenting).

Judge Ripple provided the necessary sixth vote for the result, on the much narrower ground that there had been a change of law that justified modification under *Rufo*. But the change of law had come not from a higher court or in some other litigation by other parties. The change of law had occurred only because Chicago itself was permitted to relitigate the *Evans* case. Doesn't that open all decrees to relitigation? Shouldn't defendant have to show a change of law as a condition to reopening the decree, instead of relitigating the decree to seek a change of law? For more on the facts and substantive issues of *Evans*, see note 3 at 803.

12. Consider the impact on *Rufo* of the Prison Litigation Reform Act.

> (2) IMMEDIATE TERMINATION OF PROSPECTIVE RELIEF—In any civil action with respect to prison conditions, a defendant or intervener shall be entitled to the immediate termination of any prospective relief if the relief was approved or granted in the absence of a finding by the court that the relief is narrowly drawn, extends no further than necessary to correct the violation of the Federal right, and is the least intrusive means necessary to correct the violation of the Federal right.
>
> (3) LIMITATION—Prospective relief shall not terminate if the court makes written findings based on the record that prospective relief remains necessary to correct a current or ongoing violation of the Federal right, extends no further than necessary to correct the violation of the Federal right, and that the prospective relief is narrowly drawn and the least intrusive means to correct the violation.

18 U.S.C. §3626(b) (Supp. II 1996).

Does this mean that defendants in *Rufo* can again reopen the case and that this time they can litigate the constitutional minimum? Is that constitutional? Congress has no power to require the reopening of final judgments. Plaut v. Spendthrift Farms, 115 S. Ct. 1446 (1995). But the Court acknowledged an exception for the application of new law to prospective relief, and the PLRA seems designed to fit within that exception.

13. The Act also seeks to prevent the entry of any more decrees like the one in *Rufo*:

> (1) CONSENT DECREES—In any civil action with respect to prison conditions, the court shall not enter or approve a consent decree unless it complies with the limitations on relief set forth in subsection (a) [setting

conditions for litigated decrees, reprinted supra at supplement to 299, following Lewis v. Casey].

(2) PRIVATE SETTLEMENT AGREEMENTS—

(A) Nothing in this section shall preclude parties from entering into a private settlement agreement that does not comply with the limitations on relief set forth in subsection (a), if the terms of that agreement are not subject to court enforcement other than the reinstatement of the civil proceeding that the agreement settled.

(B) Nothing in this section shall preclude any party claiming that a private settlement agreement has been breached from seeking in State court any remedy available under State law.

18 U.S.C. §3626(c) (Supp. II 1996).

Is this statute constitutional if *Rufo* is good law on the power to enforce settlements that go beyond constitutional minima? On one view, it simply enacts a rule of procedure, which Congress plainly has power to do. See generally Title 28 of the United States Code. The Supreme Court promulgates the most familiar rules of procedure only because Congress so directed in the Rules Enabling Act, 28 U.S.C. §2071 et seq. (1994), and these rules are subject to congressional override.

But on another view, this section raises serious questions of separation of powers. Does it attempt to control the bases of judicial judgment by a means other than changing the substantive law applicable to a case? Does it deprive the courts of a power essential to their functioning? If they cannot enter judgments based on consent, must they try every case that is filed? Could the courts function if this statute applied generally, instead of being confined to prisoner cases seeking prospective relief?

Is this statute constitutional if the plurality opinion in *Evans* is good law? Note that the statute goes beyond *Evans* by taking away the power to compromise "genuine uncertainties."

Can the court and parties evade the statute as currently drafted? Can parties who want to settle consent to the necessary findings, or stipulate to facts sufficient to support them? If the underlying litigation presented a real case or controversy, would such stipulations be collusive in any sense different from any other settlement?

14. Is there any reason for plaintiffs to accept a settlement that defendant can walk away from at any time, leaving plaintiff with nothing but a right to pursue his complaint? A suit for breach of the settlement contract could provide a real remedy in theory, but may have little value in fact. At least some states have not waived sovereign immunity for

breach of contract, and most (possibly all, but I haven't checked) of those who do waive immunity consent only to damages and not to specific performance. A contract action for substantial damages would give a plaintiff class leverage, but it is fair to doubt that state courts would award substantial damages to prisoners for breach of a contract to improve prison conditions. Nor do many state trial judges have the resources or a tradition in state law that would enable them to supervise structural relief in the guise of specific performance of a contract even if state law permitted them to try.

Page 344. At the end of the chapter, add:

4. A Recent Synthesis

MISSOURI v. JENKINS

115 S. Ct. 2038 (1995)

CHIEF JUSTICE REHNQUIST delivered the opinion of the Court. . . .

I . . .

This case has been before the same United States District Judge since 1977. In that year, the Kansas City Missouri School District (KCMSD), the school board, and the children of two school board members brought suit against the State and other defendants. Plaintiffs alleged that the State, the surrounding suburban school districts (SSDs), and various federal agencies had caused and perpetuated a system of racial segregation in the schools of the Kansas City metropolitan area. The District Court realigned the KCMSD as a nominal defendant and certified as a class, present and future KCMSD students. The KCMSD brought a cross-claim against the State for its failure to eliminate the vestiges of its prior dual school system.

After a trial that lasted 7½ months, the District Court dismissed the case against the federal defendants and the SSDs, but determined that the State and the KCMSD were liable for an intradistrict violation, i.e., they had operated a segregated school system within the KCMSD. 593 F. Supp. 1485 (W.D. Mo. 1984). The District Court determined that prior to 1954 "Missouri mandated segregated schools for black and white children." Id. at 1490. Furthermore, the KCMSD and the State had failed in their affirmative obligations to eliminate the vestiges of the State's dual school system within the KCMSD.

In June 1985, the District Court issued its first remedial order and established as its goal the "elimination of all vestiges of state imposed segregation." 639 F. Supp. 19, 23 (W.D. Mo. 1985). The District Court determined that "[s]egregation ha[d] caused a system wide *reduction* in student achievement in the schools of the KCMSD." Id. at 24. The District Court made no particularized findings regarding the extent that student achievement had been reduced or what portion of that reduction was attributable to segregation. The District Court also identified 25 schools within the KCMSD that had enrollments of 90 percent or more black students.

The District Court, pursuant to plans submitted by the KCMSD and the State, ordered a wide range of quality education programs for all students attending the KCMSD. . . .

The District Court also ordered programs to expand educational opportunities for all KCMSD students: full-day kindergarten; expanded summer school; before- and after-school tutoring; and an early childhood development program. Finally, the District Court implemented a state-funded "effective schools" program that consisted of substantial yearly cash grants to each of the schools within the KCMSD. . . .

The total cost for these quality education programs has exceeded $220 million. . . .

In November 1986, the District Court approved a comprehensive magnet school . . . plan . . . [E]very senior high school, every middle school, and one-half of the elementary schools were converted into magnet schools. The District Court adopted the magnet-school program to "provide a greater educational opportunity to *all* KCMSD students," and because it believed "that the proposed magnet plan [was] so attractive that it would draw non-minority students from the private schools who have abandoned or avoided the KCMSD, and draw in additional non-minority students from the suburbs." . . . Since its inception, the magnet school program has operated at a cost, including magnet transportation, in excess of $448 million. . . .

In formulating its capital-improvements plan, the District Court dismissed as "irrelevant" the "State's argument that the present condition of the facilities [was] not traceable to unlawful segregation." 639 F. Supp. at 40. Instead, the District Court focused on its responsibility to "remed[y] the vestiges of segregation" and to "implemen[t] a desegregation plan which w[ould] maintain and attract non-minority members." Id. at 41. . . .

In September 1987, the District Court adopted, for the most part, KCMSD's long-range capital improvements plan . . . 672 F. Supp. 400, 408 (W.D. Mo. 1987). The plan called for the renovation of approximately 55 schools, the closure of 18 facilities, and the construction of 17 new schools. The District Court rejected what it referred to as the "'patch and repair' approach proposed by the State" because it "would not achieve suburban comparability or the visual attractiveness sought by the Court . . ." Id. at 404. . . .[T]he total cost of capital improvements ordered has soared to over $540 million. . . .

[T]he District Court has ordered salary assistance to all but three of the approximately 5,000 KCMSD employees. The total cost of this component of the desegregation remedy since 1987 is over $200 million. . . .

The annual cost per pupil at the KCMSD far exceeds that of the neighboring SSDs or of any school district in Missouri. . . . [T]he desegregation costs . . . are approaching an annual cost of $200 million. These massive expenditures have financed

> high schools in which every classroom will have air conditioning, an alarm system, and 15 microcomputers; a 2,000-square-foot planetarium; green houses and vivariums; a 25-acre farm with an air-conditioned meeting room for 104 people; a Model United Nations wired for language translation; broadcast capable radio and television studios with an editing and animation lab; a temperature controlled art gallery; movie editing and screening rooms; a 3,500-square-foot dust-free diesel mechanics room; 1,875-square-foot elementary school animal rooms for use in a zoo project; swimming pools; and numerous other facilities.

Missouri v. Jenkins, 495 U.S. 33, 77 (1990) (Kennedy, J., concurring). . . .

II

With this background, we turn to the present controversy. First, the State has challenged the District Court's requirement that it fund salary increases for KCMSD instructional and noninstructional staff. The State claimed that funding for salaries was beyond the scope of the District Court's remedial authority. Second, the State has challenged the District

Court's order requiring it to continue to fund the remedial quality education programs for the 1992-1993 school year. The State contended that under Freeman v. Pitts, 503 U.S. 467 (1992), it had achieved partial unitary status with respect to the quality education programs already in place. As a result, the State argued that the District Court should have relieved it of responsibility for funding those programs.

The District Court rejected the State's arguments. . . .

The Court of Appeals . . . affirmed. 11 F.3d 755 (8th Cir. 1993). . . . [I]t observed that "[i]n addition to compensating the victims, the remedy in this case was also designed to reverse white flight by offering superior educational opportunities." Id. . . . It found significant the District Court's determination that although "there had been a trend of improvement in academic achievement, . . . the school district was far from reaching its maximum potential because KCMSD is still at or below national norms at many grade levels." Id. at 761-62. . . .

III . . .

[I]n *Milliken I*, we held that a District Court had exceeded its authority in fashioning interdistrict relief where the surrounding school districts had not themselves been guilty of any constitutional violation. We said that a desegregation remedy "is necessarily designed, as all remedies are, to restore the victims of discriminatory conduct to the position they would have occupied in the absence of such conduct." 418 U.S. at 746. . . .

Because "federal supervision of local school systems was intended as a temporary measure to remedy past discrimination," Board of Education v. Dowell, 498 U.S. 237, 247 (1991), we also have considered the showing that must be made by a school district operating under a desegregation order for complete or partial relief from that order. In *Freeman*, we stated that

> [a]mong the factors which must inform the sound discretion of the court in ordering partial withdrawal are the following: [1] whether there has been full and satisfactory compliance with the decree in those aspects of the system where supervision is to be withdrawn; [2] whether retention of judicial control is necessary or practicable to achieve compliance with the decree in other facets of the school system; and [3] whether the school district has demonstrated, to the public and to the parents and students of the once disfavored race, its good-faith commitment to the whole of the courts' decree and to

> those provisions of the law and the Constitution that were the predicate for judicial intervention in the first instance.

503 U.S. at 491. The ultimate inquiry is "'whether the [constitutional violator] ha[s] complied in good faith with the desegregation decree since it was entered, and whether the vestiges of past discrimination ha[ve] been eliminated to the extent practicable.'" Id. at 492, (quoting *Dowell*, 498 U.S. at 249-250). . . .

The State argues that the order approving salary increases is beyond the District Court's authority because it was crafted to serve an "interdistrict goal," in spite of the fact that the constitutional violation in this case is "intradistrict" in nature. "[T]he nature of the desegregation remedy is to be determined by the nature and scope of the constitutional violation." *Milliken II*, 433 U.S. at 280. The proper response to an intradistrict violation is an intradistrict remedy, that serves to eliminate the racial identity of the schools within the affected school district by eliminating, as far as practicable, the vestiges of de jure segregation in all facets of their operations.

Here, the District Court has found, and the Court of Appeals has affirmed, that this case involved no interdistrict constitutional violation that would support interdistrict relief. Thus, the proper response by the District Court should have been to eliminate to the extent practicable the vestiges of prior de jure segregation within the KCMSD: a system-wide reduction in student achievement and the existence of 25 racially identifiable schools with a population of over 90% black students.

The District Court and Court of Appeals, however, have felt that because the KCMSD's enrollment remained 68.3% black, a purely intradistrict remedy would be insufficient. But, as noted in *Milliken I*, we have rejected the suggestion "that schools which have a majority of Negro students are not 'desegregated' whatever the racial makeup of the school district's population and however neutrally the district lines have been drawn and administered." 418 U.S. at 747 n.22; see *Milliken II*, 433 U.S. at 280 n.14 ("[T]he Court has consistently held that the Constitution is not violated by racial imbalance in the schools, without more").

Instead of seeking to remove the racial identity of the various schools within the KCMSD, the District Court has set out on a program to create a school district that was equal to or superior to the surrounding SSDs. Its remedy has focused on "desegregative attractiveness," coupled with "suburban comparability." . . .

The purpose of desegregative attractiveness has been not only to remedy the system-wide reduction in student achievement, but also to attract nonminority students not presently enrolled in the KCMSD. . . .

But this interdistrict goal is beyond the scope of the intradistrict violation identified by the District Court. . . . [T]he District Court has devised a remedy to accomplish indirectly what it admittedly lacks the remedial authority to mandate directly: the interdistrict transfer of students. . . .

What we meant in *Milliken I* by an interdistrict violation was a violation that caused segregation between adjoining districts. Nothing in *Milliken I* suggests that the District Court in that case could have circumvented the limits on its remedial authority by requiring the State of Michigan, a constitutional violator, to implement a magnet program designed to achieve the same interdistrict transfer of students that we held was beyond its remedial authority. Here, the District Court has done just that: created a magnet district of the KCMSD in order to serve the interdistrict goal of attracting nonminority students from the surrounding SSDs and redistributing them within the KCMSD. The District Court's pursuit of "desegregative attractiveness" is beyond the scope of its broad remedial authority.

Respondents argue that the District Court's reliance upon desegregative attractiveness is justified in light of the District Court's statement that segregation has "led to white flight from the KCMSD to suburban districts." The lower courts' "findings" as to "white flight" are both inconsistent [with the finding of no interdistrict violation], and inconsistent with the typical supposition, bolstered here by the record evidence, that "white flight" may result from desegregation, not de jure segregation. . . .

The record here does not support the District Court's reliance on "white flight" as a justification for a permissible expansion of its intradistrict remedial authority through its pursuit of desegregative attractiveness.

Justice Souter claims that our holding effectively overrules Hills v. Gautreaux, 425 U.S. 284 (1976). In *Gautreaux*, the Federal Department of Housing and Urban Development (HUD) was found to have participated, along with a local housing agency, in establishing and maintaining a racially segregated public housing program. After the Court of Appeals ordered "'the adoption of a comprehensive metropolitan area plan,'" id. at 291, we granted certiorari to consider the "permissibility in the light of [*Milliken I*] of 'inter-district relief for discrimination in public housing in the absence of a finding of an inter-district violation.'" Id. at 292. Because the "relevant geographic area for the purposes of the [plaintiffs'] housing options [was] the Chicago housing market, not the Chicago city limits," id. at 299, we concluded that "a metropolitan area remedy . . . [was] not impermissible as a matter of law," id. at 306. . . .

[W]e cautioned that our holding "should not be interpreted as requiring a metropolitan area order." Id. at 306. . . .

Our decision today is fully consistent with *Gautreaux*. A district court seeking to remedy an *intra*district violation that has not "directly caused" significant interdistrict effects, *Milliken I*, 418 U.S. at 744-745, exceeds its remedial authority if it orders a remedy with an interdistrict purpose. This conclusion follows directly from *Milliken II* . . . , where we reaffirmed the bedrock principle that "federal-court decrees exceed appropriate limits if they are aimed at eliminating a condition that does not violate the Constitution or does not flow from such a violation." 433 U.S. at 282. . . .

The District Court's pursuit of "desegregative attractiveness" cannot be reconciled with our cases placing limitations on a district court's remedial authority. It is certainly theoretically possible that the greater the expenditure per pupil within the KCMSD, the more likely it is that some unknowable number of nonminority students not presently attending schools in the KCMSD will choose to enroll in those schools. Under this reasoning, however, every increased expenditure, whether it be for teachers, noninstructional employees, books, or buildings, will make the KCMSD in some way more attractive, and thereby perhaps induce nonminority students to enroll in its schools. But this rationale is not susceptible to any objective limitation. Cf. *Milliken II*, 433 U.S. at 280 (remedial decree "must be designed as nearly as possible 'to restore the victims of discriminatory conduct to the position they would have occupied in the absence of such conduct'"). This case provides numerous examples demonstrating the limitless authority of the District Court operating under this rationale. . . .

Nor are there limits to the duration of the District Court's involvement. The expenditures per pupil in the KCMSD currently far exceed those in the neighboring SSDs. Sixteen years after this litigation began, the District Court recognized that the KCMSD has yet to offer a viable method of financing the "wonderful school system being built." Each additional program ordered by the District Court—and financed by the

State—to increase the "desegregative attractiveness" of the school district makes the KCMSD more and more dependent on additional funding from the State; in turn, the greater the KCMSD's dependence on state funding, the greater its reliance on continued supervision by the District Court. But our cases recognize that local autonomy of school districts is a vital national tradition, and that a district court must strive to restore state and local authorities to the control of a school system operating in compliance with the Constitution.

Similar considerations lead us to conclude that the District Court's order requiring the State to continue to fund the quality education programs because student achievement levels were still "at or below national norms at many grade levels" cannot be sustained. . . .

Our review in this respect is needlessly complicated because the District Court made no findings in its order approving continued funding of the quality education programs. . . . [T]he Court of Appeals . . . attempted to assemble an adequate record from the District Court's statements from the bench and subsequent orders. In one such order relied upon by the Court of Appeals, the District Court stated that the KCMSD had not reached anywhere close to its "maximum potential because the District is still at or below national norms at many grade levels."

But this clearly is not the appropriate test to be applied in deciding whether a previously segregated district has achieved partially unitary status. The basic task of the District Court is to decide whether the reduction in achievement by minority students attributable to prior de jure segregation has been remedied to the extent practicable. Under our precedents, the State and the KCMSD are "entitled to a rather precise statement of [their] obligations under a desegregation decree." *Freeman*, 503 U.S. at 246. Although the District Court has determined that "[s]egregation has caused a system wide *reduction* in achievement in the schools of the KCMSD," 639 F. Supp. at 24, it never has identified the incremental effect that segregation has had on minority student achievement or the specific goals of the quality education programs. Cf. *Dayton I.*

In reconsidering this order, the District Court should apply our three-part test from *Freeman*, 503 U.S. at 491. . . . As all the parties agree that improved achievement on test scores is not necessarily required for the State to achieve partial unitary status as to the quality education programs, the District Court should sharply limit, if not dispense with, its reliance on this factor. Just as demographic changes independent of de jure segregation will affect the racial composition of student assignments, so too will numerous external factors beyond the control of the KCMSD and the State affect minority student achievement. So long as these external factors are not the result of segregation, they do not figure in the remedial calculus. . . .

The District Court also should consider that many goals of its quality education plan already have been attained: the KCMSD now is equipped with "facilities and opportunities not available anywhere else in the country." . . . [T]he remedial quality education program should be tailored to remedy the injuries suffered by the victims of prior de jure segregation. Minority students in kindergarten through grade 7 in the KCMSD always have attended AAA-rated schools; minority students in the KCMSD that previously attended schools rated below AAA have since received remedial education programs for a period of up to seven years.

On remand, the District Court must bear in mind that its end purpose is not only "to remedy the violation" to the extent practicable, but also "to restore state and local authorities to the control of a school system that is operating in compliance with the Constitution." *Freeman*, 503 U.S. at 489.

The judgment of the Court of Appeals is reversed. . . .

JUSTICE O'CONNOR, concurring. . . .

[T]he Court's resolution of the dispute comports with *Gautreaux*. . . . *Gautreaux* . . . does not eliminate the requirement of *Milliken I* that [remedies that go beyond the boundaries of the constitutional violator are] permissible only upon a showing that the intradistrict constitutional violation produced significant interdistrict segregative effects; if anything, our opinion repeatedly affirmed that principle. More important for our purposes here, *Gautreaux* in no way contravenes the underlying principle that the scope of desegregation remedies, even those that are solely intradistrict, is "determined by the nature and extent of the constitutional violation." *Milliken I*, 418 U.S. at 744, (citing *Swann*, 402 U.S. at 16). . . .

As an initial matter, *Gautreaux* itself may not even have concerned a case of interdistrict relief, at least not in the sense that *Milliken I* and other school desegregation cases have understood it. Our opinion made clear that [HUD's] authority . . . extends beyond the Chicago city limits, and that HUD's own administrative practice treated the Chicago metropolitan area as an undifferentiated whole. Thus, "[t]he relevant geographic area for purposes of the respondents' housing options is the Chicago housing market, not the Chicago city limits." 425 U.S. at 299. . . .

Here, where the District Court found that KCMSD students attended schools separated by their race and that facilities have "literally rotted," 672 F. Supp. at 411, the District Court of course should order restorations and remedies that would place previously segregated black KCMSD students at par with their white KCMSD counterparts. . . .

What the District Court did in this case . . ., and how it transgressed the constitutional bounds of its remedial powers, is to make desegregative attractiveness the underlying goal of its remedy for the specific purpose of reversing the trend of white flight. However troubling that trend may be, remedying it is within the District Court's authority only if it is "directly caused by the constitutional violation." 418 U.S. at 745. . . . [T]he District Court cannot order remedies seeking to rectify regional demographic trends that go beyond the nature and scope of the constitutional violation. . . .

For these reasons, I join the opinion of the Court.

JUSTICE THOMAS, concurring.

It never ceases to amaze me that the courts are so willing to assume that anything that is predominantly black must be inferior. Instead of focusing on remedying the harm done to those black schoolchildren injured by segregation, the District Court here sought to convert the KCMSD into a "magnet district" that would reverse the "white flight" caused by desegregation. In this respect, I join the Court's decision concerning the two remedial issues presented for review. . . .

I

A

The mere fact that a school is black does not mean that it is the product of a constitutional violation. . . .

[T]he District Court inferred a continuing constitutional violation from two primary facts: the existence of de jure segregation in the KCMSD prior to 1954, and the existence of de facto segregation today. . . . For the District Court, it followed that the KCMSD had not dismantled the dual system entirely. The District Court also concluded that . . . the dual system still exerted "lingering effects" upon KCMSD black students, whose "general attitude of inferiority" produced "low achievement . . . which ultimately limits employment opportunities and causes poverty." Id. at 1492.

Without more, the District Court's findings could not have supported a finding of liability against the state. . . . [T]he existence of one-race schools is not by itself an indication that the State is practicing segregation. The continuing "racial isolation" of schools after de jure segregation has ended may well reflect voluntary housing choices or other private decisions. Here, for instance, the demography of the entire KCMSD has changed considerably since 1954. Though blacks accounted for only 18.9% of KCMSD's enrollment in 1954, by 1983-1984 the school district was 67.7% black. That certain schools are overwhelmingly black in a district that is now more than two-thirds black is hardly a sure sign of intentional state action.

In search of intentional state action, the District Court linked the State and the dual school system of 1984 in two ways. First, the Court found that . . . laws from the Jim Crow era created "an atmosphere in which . . . private white individuals could justify their bias and prejudice against blacks," with the possible result that private realtors, bankers, and insurers engaged in more discriminatory activities than would otherwise have occurred. 593 F. Supp. at 1503. But the District Court itself acknowledged that the State's alleged encouragement of private discrimination was a fairly tenuous basis for finding liability. The District Court therefore rested the State's liability on the simple fact that the State had intentionally created the dual school system before 1954, and had failed to fulfill "its affirmative duty of disestablishing a dual school system subsequent to 1954." Id. at 1504. According to the District Court, the schools whose student bodies were more than 90% black constituted "vestiges" of the prior de jure segregation, which the State and the KCMSD had an obligation to eliminate. Id. at 1504, 1506. Later, . . . the District Court added that a "system wide reduction in student achievement in the schools of . . . KCMSD" was also a vestige of the prior de jure segregation. 639 F. Supp. at 24 (emphasis deleted).[1] In a subsequent

1. It appears that the low achievement levels were never properly attributed to any discriminatory actions on the part of the State or of KCMSD. The District Court simply

order, the District Court indicated that post-1954 "white flight" was another vestige of the pre-1954 segregated system.

In order for a "vestige" to supply the ground for an exercise of remedial authority, it must be clearly traceable to the dual school system. . . .

When a district court holds the State liable for discrimination almost 30 years after the last official state action, it must do more than show that there are schools with high black populations or low test scores. . . . [W]here, as here, the finding of liability comes so late in the day, I would think it incumbent upon the District Court to explain how more recent social or demographic phenomena did not cause the "vestiges." This the District Court did not do.

B

Without a basis in any real finding of intentional government action, . . . the [district] court has "indulged the presumption, often irrebuttable in practice, that a presently observed [racial] imbalance has been proximately caused by intentional state action during the prior de jure era." United States v. Fordice, 112 S. Ct. 2727, 2744 (Thomas, J., concurring) (citing *Dayton II* and *Keyes*). In effect, the court found that racial imbalances constituted an ongoing constitutional violation that continued to inflict harm on black students. This position appears to rest upon the idea that any school that is black is inferior, and that blacks cannot succeed without the benefit of the company of whites.

The District Court's willingness to adopt such stereotypes stemmed from a misreading of our earliest school desegregation case. In *Brown I*, the Court noted several psychological and sociological studies purporting to show that de jure segregation harmed black students by generating "a feeling of inferiority" in them. . . .

It is clear that the District Court misunderstood . . . *Brown I*. *Brown I* did not say that "racially isolated" schools were inherently inferior; the harm that it identified was tied purely to de jure segregation, not de facto segregation. . . .

---

found that the KCMSD's test scores were below national norms in reading and mathematics. Without more, these statistics are meaningless.

Regardless of the relative quality of the schools, segregation violated the Constitution because the State classified students based on their race. Of course, segregation additionally harmed black students by relegating them to schools with substandard facilities and resources. But neutral policies, such as local school assignments, do not offend the Constitution when individual private choices concerning work or residence produce schools with high black populations. The Constitution does not prevent individuals from choosing to live together, to work together, or to send their children to school together, so long as the State does not interfere with their choices on the basis of race.

Given that desegregation has not produced the predicted leaps forward in black educational achievement, there is no reason to think that black students cannot learn as well when surrounded by members of their own race as when they are in an integrated environment. Indeed, it may very well be that what has been true for historically black colleges is true for black middle and high schools. Despite their origins in "the shameful history of state-enforced segregation," these institutions can be "'both a source of pride to blacks who have attended them and a source of hope to black families who want the benefits of . . . learning for their children.'" *Fordice*, 112 S. Ct. at 2746 (Thomas, J., concurring). Because of their "distinctive histories and traditions," id. at 2746, black schools can function as the center and symbol of black communities, and provide examples of independent black leadership, success, and achievement. . . .

"Racial isolation" itself is not a harm; only state-enforced segregation is. . . .

II . . .

Not only did the court subscribe to a theory of injury that was predicated on black inferiority, it also married this concept of liability to our expansive approach to remedial powers. We have given the federal courts the freedom to use any measure necessary to reverse problems — such as racial isolation or low educational achievement — that have proven stubbornly resistant to government policies. . . .

A . . .

I assume for purposes of this case that the remedial authority of the federal courts is inherent in the "judicial Power," as there is no general equitable remedial power expressly granted by the Constitution or by statute. As with any inherent judicial power, however, we ought to be reluctant to approve its aggressive or extravagant use . . .

Motivated by our worthy desire to eradicate segregation, however, we have disregarded this principle and given the courts unprecedented authority to shape a remedy in equity. . . .

Our impatience with the pace of desegregation and with the lack of a good-faith effort on the part of school boards led us to approve . . . extraordinary remedial measures. But such powers should have been temporary and used only to overcome the widespread resistance to the dictates of the Constitution. . . .

B . . .

The available historical records suggest that the Framers did not intend federal equitable remedies to reach as broadly as we have permitted. . . .

Blackstone emphasized that courts of equity must be governed by rules and precedents no less than the courts of law. "[I]f a court of equity were still at sea, and floated upon the occasional opinion which the judge who happened to preside might entertain of conscience in every particular case, the inconvenience that would arise from this uncertainty, would be a worse evil than any hardship that could follow from rules too strict and inflexible." 3 William Blackstone, Commentaries 440 (1768). . . .

So cautioned, the Framers approached equity with suspicion. . . . Anti-Federalists attacked the Constitution's extension of the federal judicial power to "Cases, in Law and Equity," . . . Said the "Federal Farmer," "by thus joining the word equity with the word law, if we mean any thing, we seem to mean to give the judge a discretionary power." Federal Farmer No. 15, January 18, 1788, in 2 The Complete Anti-Federalist 322 (Herbert Storing ed. 1981). . . . Another Anti-Federalist, Brutus, argued that the equity power would allow federal courts to "explain the constitution according to the reasoning spirit of it, without being confined to the words or letter." Brutus No. 11, January 31, 1788, id. at 419. This, predicted Brutus, would result in the growth of federal power and the "entire subversion of the legislative, executive and judicial powers of the individual states." Id. at 420. . . .

Answering the Anti-Federalist challenge in The Federalist Papers, Alexander Hamilton . . . argued (as Blackstone had in describing the English equity courts) that rules and established practices would limit and control the judicial power. . . . Hamilton emphasized that "[t]he great and primary use of a court of equity is to give relief in extraordinary cases," and that "the principles by which that relief is governed are now reduced to a regular system." The Federalist No. 83, at 569 & n. (J. Cooke ed. 1961). . . .

[T]here is no early record of the exercise of broad remedial powers. Certainly there were no "structural injunctions" issued by the federal courts, nor were there any examples of continuing judicial supervision and management of governmental institutions. . . . At the very least, given the Federalists' public explanation during the ratification of the federal equity power, we should exercise the power to impose equitable remedies only sparingly, subject to clear rules guiding its use.

C

Two clear restraints on the use of the equity power—federalism and the separation of powers—derive from the very form of our Government. Federal courts should pause before using their inherent equitable powers to intrude into the proper sphere of the States. . . . A structural reform decree eviscerates a State's discretionary authority over its own program and budgets and forces state officials to reallocate state resources and funds to the desegregation plan at the expense of other citizens, other government programs, and other institutions not represented in court. . . .

The separation of powers imposes additional restraints on the judiciary's exercise of its remedial powers. . . . [W]hat the federal courts cannot do at the federal level they cannot do against the States; in either case, Article III courts are constrained by the inherent constitutional limitations on their powers. There simply are certain things that courts, in order to remain courts, cannot and should not do. There is no difference between courts running school systems or prisons and courts running executive branch agencies.

In this case, not only did the district court exercise the legislative power to tax, it also engaged in budgeting, staffing, and educational decisions, in judgments about the location and aesthetic quality of the schools, and in administrative oversight and monitoring. These functions involve a legislative or executive, rather than a judicial, power. . . .

[W]e must impose more precise standards and guidelines on the federal equitable power, not only to restore predictability to the law and reduce judicial discretion, but also to ensure that constitutional remedies are actually targeted toward those who have been injured.

D . . .

When the standard of review is as vague as whether "Federal-court decrees . . . directly address and relate to the constitutional violation," *Milliken II*, 433 U.S. at 281-282, it is difficult to ever find a remedial order "unreasonable." Such criteria provide District Courts with little guidance, and provide appellate courts few principles with which to review trial court decisions. If the standard reduces to what one believes is a "fair" remedy, or what vaguely appears to be a good "fit" between violation and remedy, then there is little hope of imposing the constraints on the equity power that the framers envisioned and that our constitutional system requires. . . .

[T]he District Court's remedial orders are in tension with two common-sense principles. First, the District Court retained jurisdiction over the implementation and modification of the remedial decree, instead of terminating its involvement after issuing its remedy. Although briefly mentioned in *Brown II* as a temporary measure to overcome local resistance to desegregation, this concept of continuing judicial involvement has permitted the District Courts to revise their remedies constantly in order to reach some broad, abstract, and often elusive goal. Not only does this approach deprive the parties of finality and a clear understanding of their responsibilities, but it also tends to inject the judiciary into the day-to-day management of institutions and local policies—a function that lies outside of our Article III competence. . . .

Wherever possible, district courts should focus their remedial discretion on devising and implementing a unified remedy in a single decree. This method would still provide the lower courts with substantial flexibility to tailor a remedy to fit a violation, and courts could employ their contempt power to ensure compliance. . . .

Second, the District Court failed to target its equitable remedies in this case specifically to cure the harm suffered by the victims of segregation. . . .

KCMSD as a whole may have experienced reduced achievement levels, but raising the test scores of the entire district is a goal that is not sufficiently tailored to restoring the victims of segregation to the position they would have occupied absent discrimination. A school district cannot be discriminated against on the basis of its race, because a school district has no race. It goes without saying that only individuals can suffer from discrimination, and only individuals can receive the remedy. . . .

In the absence of special circumstances, the remedy for de jure segregation ordinarily should not include educational programs for students who were not in school (or were even alive) during the period of segregation. . . .

JUSTICE SOUTER, with whom JUSTICES STEVENS, GINSBURG, and BREYER join, dissenting. . . .

I . . .

After *Brown I*, neither the State nor the KCMSD moved to dismantle [the] system of separate education "root and branch," despite their affirmative obligation to do that under the Constitution. "Instead, the [KCMSD] chose to operate some completely segregated schools and some integrated ones," 593 F. Supp. at 1492, using devices like optional attendance zones and liberal transfer policies to "allo[w] attendance patterns to continue on a segregated basis." Id. at 1494. . . . Because the State and the KCMSD intentionally created this segregated system of education, and subsequently failed to correct it, the District Court concluded that the State and the district had "defaulted in their obligation to uphold the Constitution." Id. at 1505.

Neither the State nor the KCMSD appealed this finding of liability, after which the District Court entered a series of remedial orders aimed at eliminating the vestiges of segregation. Since the District Court found that segregation had caused, among other things, "a system wide *reduction* in student achievement in the schools of the KCMSD," 639 F. Supp. at 24, it ordered the adoption, starting in 1985, of a series of remedial programs to raise educational performance. . . .

II

A

The test score question as it comes to us is one of word play, not substance. . . . [N]one of the District Court's or Court of Appeals's opinions or orders requires a certain level of test scores before unitary status can be found, or indicates that test scores are the only thing standing between the State and a finding of unitary status as to the KCMSD's *Milliken II* programs. . . .

If, then, test scores do not explain why there was no finding of unitary status as to the *Milliken II* programs, one may ask what does explain it. The answer is quite straightforward. . . . [T]he State did not attempt to make the showing required for that relief. . . .

[T]he State failed even to allege its compliance with two of the three prongs of the *Freeman* test.

The State did not claim that implementation of the *Milliken II* component of the decree had remedied the reduction in student achievement in the KCMSD to the extent practicable; it simply argued that various *Milliken II* programs had been implemented. . . .

Nor did the State focus on its own good faith in complying with the District Court's decree; it emphasized instead the district's commitment to the decree and to the constitutional provisions on which the decree rested. . . .

Thus, it was the State's failure to meet or even to recognize its burden under *Freeman* that led the Court of Appeals to reject the suggestion that it make a finding of partial unitary status as to the district's *Milliken II* education programs. . . . 11 F.3d at 764-765. . . .

[A]ll parties to this case agree that it would be error to require that the students in a school district attain the national average test score as a prerequisite to a finding of partial unitary status, if only because all sorts of causes independent of the vestiges of past school segregation might stand in the way of the goal. That said, test scores will clearly be relevant in determining whether the improvement programs have cured a deficiency in student achievement to the practicable extent. The District Court has noted . . . that while students' scores have shown a trend of improvement, they remain at or below national norms. The significance of this fact is subject to assessment. Depending, of course, on other facts developed in the course of unitary status proceedings, the improvement to less than the national average might reasonably be taken to show that education programs are having a good effect on student achievement, and that further improvement can be expected. On the other hand, if test score changes were shown to have flattened out, that might suggest the impracticability of any additional remedial progress. . . .

B . . .

[T]he District Court did not ground its orders of salary increases solely on the goal of attracting students back to the KCMSD. From the start, the District Court has consistently treated salary increases as an important element in remedying the systemwide reduction in student achievement resulting from segregation in the KCMSD. . . . [T]he Court does not question this remedial goal, which we expressly approved in *Milliken II*. The only issue, then, is whether the salary increases ordered by the District Court have been reasonably related to achieving that goal, keeping in mind the broad discretion enjoyed by the District Court in exercising its equitable powers. . . .

[A]dopting the state's position and discontinuing desegregation funding for salary levels would result in their abrupt drop to 1986-1987 levels, with the resulting disparity between teacher pay in the district and the nationwide level increasing to as much as 40-45 percent, and a mass exodus of competent employees likely taking place. Faced with this evidence, the District Court found that continued desegregation funding of salaries, and small increases in those salaries over time, were essential to the successful implementation of its remedial scheme, including the elevation of student achievement. . . .

There is nothing exceptionable in the lower courts' findings about the relationship between salaries and the District Court's remedial objectives, and certainly nothing in the record suggests obvious error as to the amounts of the increases ordered. If it is tempting to question the place of salary increases for administrative and maintenance personnel in a desegregation order, the Court of Appeals addressed the temptation in specifically affirming the District Court's finding that such personnel are critical to the success of the desegregation effort, and did so in the circumstances of a district whose schools have been plagued by leaking roofs, defective lighting, and reeking lavatories. . . .

Indeed, the Court does not question the District Court's salary orders insofar as they relate to the objective of raising the level of student achievement in the KCMSD, but rather overlooks that basis for the orders altogether. The Court suggests that the District Court rested its approval of salary increases only on the object of drawing students into the district's schools, and rejects the increases for that reason. It seems clear, however, that the District Court and the Court of Appeals both viewed the salary orders as serving two complementary but distinct purposes, and to the extent that the District Court concludes on remand that its salary orders are justified by reference to the quality of education alone, nothing in the Court's opinion precludes those orders from remaining in effect.

III . . .

[T]he District Court did not mean by an "intradistrict violation" what the Court apparently means by it today. The District Court meant that the violation within the KCMSD had not led to segregation outside of it, and that no other school districts had played a part in the violation. It did not mean that the violation had not produced effects of any sort beyond the district. . . .[4] . . .

A

[T]he District Court and the Court of Appeals concurred in finding that "the preponderance of black students in the [KCMSD] was due to the State and KCMSD's constitutional violations, which caused white flight. . . ." 855 F.2d at 1302. . . .

The Court, however, rejects the findings . . . [I]t relies on a "contradiction" that is not an obvious contradiction at all, and on an arbitrary "supposition" that "'white flight' may result from desegregation, not de jure segregation" . . .

There is . . . no contradiction between [the finding of no interdistrict segregative effect] and the . . . findings about white flight: while white

4. [Attracting students from other districts] was not the only, or even the principal, purpose of the magnet schools. The District Court found that magnet schools would assist in remedying the deficiencies in student achievement in the KCMSD. Moreover . . . the program is primarily aimed . . . at drawing back children who attend private schools while living within the geographical confines of the KCMSD, whose population remains majority white. . . . [M]uch of the Court's opinion is of little significance to the case before it.

flight would have produced significant effects in other school districts, in the form of greatly increased numbers of white students, those effects would not have been segregative beyond the KCMSD, as the departing students were absorbed into wholly unitary systems.

Without the contradiction, the Court has nothing . . . but its supposition that flight results from integration, not segregation. The supposition, and the distinction on which it rests, are untenable. . . . [T]here is in fact no break in the chain of causation linking the effects of desegregation with those of segregation. There would be no desegregation orders and no remedial plans without prior unconstitutional segregation as the occasion for issuing and adopting them, and an adverse reaction to a desegregation order is traceable in fact to the segregation that is subject to the remedy. . . .

The unreality of the Court's categorical distinction can be illustrated by some examples. There is no dispute that before the District Court's remedial plan was placed into effect the schools in the unreformed segregated system were physically a shambles. . . . The cost of turning this shambles into habitable schools was enormous . . . Property-tax-paying parents of white children, seeing the handwriting on the wall in 1985, could well have decided that the inevitable cost of clean-up would produce an intolerable tax rate and could have moved to escape it. The District Court's remedial orders had not yet been put in place. Was the white flight caused by segregation or desegregation? The distinction has no significance. . . .

All the judges who spoke to the issue below concluded that segregated schooling in the KCMSD contributed to the exodus of white students from the district. Among them were not only the judges most familiar with the record of this litigation . . . but also the five judges who dissented from the denial of rehearing en banc in the Court of Appeals (whose opinion the majority does not hesitate to rely on for other purposes) . . .

B . . .

We are not dealing here with an interdistrict remedy in the sense that *Milliken I* used the term. In the *Milliken I* litigation, the District Court had ordered 53 surrounding school districts to be consolidated with the Detroit school system, and mandatory busing to be started within the enlarged district, even though the court had not found that any of the suburban districts had acted in violation of the Constitution. . . . It was this imposition of remedial measures on more than the one wrongdoing school district that we termed an "interdistrict remedy". . . . And it was just this subjection to court order of school districts not shown to have violated the Constitution that we deemed to be in error:

> Before the boundaries of separate and autonomous school districts may be set aside by consolidating the separate units for remedial purposes or by imposing a cross-district remedy, it must first be shown that there has been a constitutional violation within one district that produces a significant segregative effect in another district. . . .

Id. at 744-745.

We did not hold, however, that any remedy that takes into account conditions outside of the district in which a constitutional violation has been committed is an "interdistrict remedy," and as such improper in the absence of an "interdistrict violation." . . .

The Court, nonetheless, reads *Milliken I* quite differently. It reads the case as categorically forbidding imposition of a remedy on a guilty district with intended consequences in a neighboring innocent district, unless the constitutional violation yielded segregative effects in that innocent district.

Today's decision therefore amounts to a redefinition of the terms of *Milliken I* and consequently to a substantial expansion of its limitation on the permissible remedies for prior segregation. . . .

Two Terms after *Milliken I*, we decided *Gautreaux*, in a unanimous opinion by Justice Stewart. The District Court . . . had found that [HUD] and the Chicago Housing Authority (CHA) had maintained a racially segregated system of public housing within the City of Chicago . . . There was no indication that the violation had produced any effects outside the city . . .

We agreed with HUD that the principles of *Milliken I* apply outside of the school desegregation context, 425 U.S. at 294 & n.11, but squarely rejected its restricted interpretation of those principles and its view of limited equitable authority to remedy segregation. We held that a district court may indeed subject a governmental perpetrator of segregative practices to an order for relief with intended consequences beyond the perpetrator's own subdivision, even in the absence of effects outside that subdivision, so long as the decree does not bind the authorities of other governmental units that are free of violations and segregative effects:

> . . . The District Court's desegregation order in *Milliken* was held to be an impermissible remedy not because it envisioned relief against a wrongdoer extending beyond the city in which the violation occurred but because it contemplated a judicial decree restructuring the operation of local governmental entities that were not implicated in any constitutional violation.

Id. at 296. . . .

Requiring a remedy outside the city in the wider metropolitan area was permissible not only because that was the area of the housing market even for people who lived within the city (thus relating the scope of the remedy to the violation suffered by the victims) but also because the trial court could order a remedy in that market without binding a governmental unit innocent of the violation and free of its effects. . . .

On its face, the District Court's magnet school concept falls entirely within the scope of equitable authority recognized in *Gautreaux*. . . . [T]he District Court has not sought to "consolidate or in any way restructure" the SSDs, id. at 305-306, or, indeed, to subject them to any remedial obligation at all.[7] The District Court's remedial measures go only to the operation and quality of schools within the KCMSD, and the burden of those measures accordingly falls only on the two proven constitutional wrongdoers in this case, the KCMSD and the State. And insofar as the District Court has ordered those violators to undertake measures to increase the KCMSD's attractiveness to students from other districts and thereby to reverse the flight attributable to their prior segregative acts, its orders do not represent an abuse of discretion, but instead appear "wholly commensurate with the 'nature and extent of the constitutional violation.'" Id. at 300, quoting *Milliken I*, 418 U.S. at 744. . . .

Gautreaux's holding is now effectively overruled, for the Court's opinion can be viewed as correct only on that assumption. . . .

I respectfully dissent.

7. Thus, the Court errs in suggesting that the District Court has sought to do here indirectly what we held the District Court could not do directly in *Milliken I*. The District Court here has not attempted, directly or indirectly, to impose any remedial measures on school districts innocent of a constitutional violation or free from its segregative effects.

JUSTICE GINSBURG, dissenting.

I join Justice Souter's illuminating dissent . . .

The Court stresses that the present remedial programs have been in place for seven years. But compared to more than two centuries of firmly entrenched official discrimination, the experience with the desegregation remedies ordered by the District Court has been evanescent. . . .

Today, the Court declares illegitimate the goal of attracting nonminority students to the [KCMSD] . . . Given the deep, inglorious history of segregation in Missouri, to curtail desegregation at this time and in this manner is an action at once too swift and too soon. Cf. App. to Pet. for Cert. A-13 (Court of Appeals noted with approval that the District Court had ordered the School District to submit plans projecting termination of court-ordered funding at alternative intervals, running from April 1993, of three, five, seven, or, at most, ten years).

MORE NOTES ON THE SCOPE OF INJUNCTIVE RELIEF

1. The principal case is *Jenkins III* in the Supreme Court. *Jenkins II* is the 1990 decision on tax increases, reprinted in the main volume at 300. *Jenkins I*, a 1989 decision on attorneys' fees, is noted in the main volume at 859 and 863.

2. *Jenkins III* is partly a decision that the relief granted exceeded the district court's power from the beginning; it is partly a decision that the state is now entitled to termination of parts of the decree that were permissible at the beginning. Much of the disagreement is over whether *Gautreaux* was principally about the scope of relief or principally about the rights of third parties. This total defeat for casebook organizational structures is inevitable in the real world of litigation. But the ambiguity inherent in prolonged cases becomes one more subject of adversary manipulation. It seems to be common ground that the burden of going forward and of persuasion turns on whether the Court characterizes the case as plaintiffs seeking additional relief or as defendants seeking termination of interim relief.

3. The majority reacted to what it thought were outlandish expenditures far in excess of anything Kansas City would have had in the absence of segregation. Note the Court's statement that the rationale of desegregative attractiveness has "no objective limitation," followed by a quotation of

the rightful position principle. Is that a stronger basis for decision than the claim that this was an interdistrict remedy for an intradistrict violation? Might *Jenkins III* have been an easy case that made bad law?

4. Does the dissent recognize any limits on the pursuit of increased academic achievement and the reversal of white flight? Improvement to the extent "practicable" suggests that the ultimate limit is the amount of money the court can raise. Proportionality, incremental harm done by the violation, and plaintiffs' position but for the wrong—are these simply irrelevant to the dissent?

5. If this massive effort to raise educational achievement is constitutionally required in Kansas City, why is it not constitutionally required in every other underachieving school system with a history of deliberate segregation? Is there any reason to believe that segregation in Kansas City had factually unique consequences? Should a billion dollar remedy be simply a discretionary choice, to be conferred or imposed on some school districts but not others depending on which judge draws the case?

6. Justice Souter suggests that the remedy can end when the improvement in test scores flattens out. Justice Ginsburg suggests the remedy should end in three to ten more years. But how can the remedy ever end without causing a disastrous collapse back to budget levels of the mid-eighties? Temporary inflation of operating budgets may be even more anomalous than temporary busing. And if ten years of remedy is "evanescent" compared to more than two centuries of official discrimination, why might thirteen or twenty years be enough?

7. Suppose the question were not how to remedy deliberate segregation by the state, but rather how to make education work in large urban school districts. Should we then be surprised that a massive effort is required? Might the plaintiffs or the district court have assumed that the two questions are the same?

CHAPTER 4

Choosing Remedies

A. SUBSTITUTIONARY OR SPECIFIC RELIEF

1. Irreplaceable Losses

Page 357. After note 5, add:

5.1. Consider Continental Airlines v. Intra Brokers, 24 F.3d 1099 (9th Cir. 1994), enjoining defendant from buying and selling nontransferable coupons that were good for a discount on plane tickets. Defendant's brokerage increased use of the coupons, which increased the number of passengers but reduced the average fare. There was no evidence whether Continental was helped or hurt on balance. The difficulty and expense of proving damages made the damage remedy inadequate.

In addition, the court said, Continental was entitled to an injunction even if it profited from increased use of the coupons. Continental was entitled to decide for itself whether the coupons should be transferrable. "There is certain harm to Continental's control of its own business, even though the harm to its profitability is unproven or perhaps immeasurable." Id. at 1105. Compare *Howell Pipeline* in note 2. Continental's "control of its business" is another example of an irreplaceable loss: If control is usurped, Continental cannot purchase replacement control on the open market.

2. Undue Hardship

Page 392. After note 4, add:

But the Supreme Court of Oklahoma has repudiated *Rock Island* and reaffirmed *Peevyhouse*. Schneberger v. Apache Corp., 890 P.2d 847 (Okla. 1994).

5. For a detailed history of *Peevyhouse*, with photographs, original documents, and interviews with the lawyers and litigants, see Judith L. Maute, Peevyhouse v. Garland Coal & Mining Co. Revisited: The Ballad of Willie and Lucille, 89 Nw. U. L. Rev. 1341 (1995).

4. Reasons of Substantive or Procedural Policy

Page 406. After note 3, add:

3.1. The Court has also held that an injunction against speech is not a prior restraint if it is not based on the content of the speech and forbids speech only in a particular time, place, or manner. Madsen v. Women's Health Center, 114 S. Ct. 2516, 2524 n.2, 2525 (1994). *Madsen* is further described supra in the supplement to 275.

B. PRELIMINARY OR PERMANENT RELIEF

Page 448. After the first paragraph of note 7, add:

The continued vitality of the rule against appealing TROs is illustrated in McGraw-Hill Companies v. Procter & Gamble Co., 116 S. Ct. 6 (1995) (Stevens, J., in chambers). McGraw-Hill, the publisher of Business Week, appealed a TRO forbidding publication of documents produced in pending litigation. The Sixth Circuit dismissed the appeal for lack of jurisdiction, and Justice Stevens refused to stay the district court's order. He doubted his own jurisdiction, and he was certain that the better course would have been a motion to dissolve the order in the district court. He noted that the TRO had been entered without the findings of fact required by Rule 65(b), and he assumed that a refusal to dissolve the TRO would have been an appealable order.

C. PROSPECTIVE OR RETROSPECTIVE RELIEF

Page 462. After note 9, add:

9.1. *Union Gas* was overruled in Seminole Tribe v. Florida, 116 S. Ct. 1114 (1996). The majority insisted that state sovereign immunity is a constitutional right of states, of which the eleventh amendment is merely an illustration, and that of course Congress cannot override constitutional rights by mere legislation under its Article I powers. The Court distinguished Fitzpatrick v. Bitzer, 427 U.S. 445 (1976), holding that §5 of the fourteenth amendment does empower Congress to authorize suits against states, because the fourteenth amendment had "fundamentally altered the balance of state and federal power struck by the Constitution." 116 S. Ct. at 1125.

Four dissenters—Stevens, Souter, Ginsburg, and Breyer—endorsed a lengthy and powerful dissent by Justice Souter. Justice Souter argued that sovereign immunity was a common law doctrine, not incorporated into the Constitution, and therefore changeable at the will of Congress, and that the eleventh amendment is only about diversity jurisdiction and that it was so intended. He argued that *Hans* was wrongly decided, but that in any event, *Hans* had not presented the question whether Congress could authorize suits against states. Thus, the Court was going far beyond *Hans* and making up a constitutional right with no basis outside the majority's preferences. Contrary to my speculation in note 5 in the main volume, he argued that already in the 1790s there were narrow grants of jurisdiction over certain categories of federal question cases, and that Congress considered but did not adopt an amendment that would have explicitly barred all suits against states in federal court. It appears that the persistent five-four split on state sovereign immunity has been re-established.

Page 462. After note 10, add:

11. *Seminole Tribe* may reduce the occasions to apply the clear-statement rule, but where it applies, the rule remains fierce. Lane v. Peña, 64 U.S.L.W. 4541 (U.S., June 20, 1996), holds that Congress did not waive immunity from suit against federal agencies that violate the Rehabilitation Act of 1973, 29 U.S.C. §794(a) (1994), although it did waive immunity from suit against federal agencies who provide financial assistance to state or private agencies that violate the Act. There is no conceivable policy rationale why federal agencies should be suable for aiding violators but not suable for their own violations. But sloppy drafting left this ambiguity open, and Justices Souter and Ginsburg joined the majority to make seven votes against waiver.

12. Many government agencies are separately incorporated. One recurring eleventh amendment issue is which of these separate agencies are treated as the state and get the state's immunity, and which are treated like local government or private corporations, without the state's immunity. The Supreme Court recently decided that the Port Authority Trans-Hudson Corp. does not have eleventh amendment immunity. Hess v. Port Authority Trans-Hudson Corp., 115 S. Ct. 394 (1994). The Port Authority is a subsidiary of an agency created by compact between New York and New Jersey; plaintiff claims to have been injured in the course of his employment on commuter trains operated by the Port Authority. The majority emphasized that neither state was liable for judgments against the Authority, and that each state necessarily surrendered some of its sovereignty when it entered an interstate compact with Congressional consent. There were four dissents.

The case illustrates some of the complexities and malpractice traps in this area. Statutes in each state waive the Port Authority's immunity from suit in both state and federal court, but subject to a one-year statute of limitations. The Supreme Court has construed the Federal Employers Liability Act to create a cause of action for injured railroad workers against states that run railroads. Hilton v. South Carolina Public Railways Commission, 502 U.S. 197 (1991). But the FELA does not override the states' immunity to suit in federal court, Welch v. Texas Department of Highways and Public Transportation, 483 U.S. 468 (1987), so suits against states, based on the FELA without more, must be filed in state court. The FELA has a three-year statute of limitations.

Hess filed suit in federal court, two years and eleven months after his injury, relying on the Port Authority's statutory waiver of immunity and the federal statute of limitations. But these were elements of two separate and somewhat incompatible theories. He could have filed suit pursuant to the state waiver, but only within one year of his injury. He could have filed suit without relying on the state waiver, but only in state court. Neither theory permitted him to file suit in federal court more than one year after the injury. He was therefore forced to argue a third completely separate theory, that the Port Authority could be sued in federal court because it had no eleventh amendment immunity in the first place. He won, but the threshold victory consumed four-and-a-half years of litigation. His case was remanded for consideration of the merits more than seven years after his alleged injury.

Page 464. After note 5, add:

6. The Court added a fifth limit in Seminole Tribe v. Florida, 116 S. Ct. 1114, 1132-1133 (1996). Where Congress has provided a detailed remedy that does not include a *Young* suit against a state official, the statutory remedy preempts the *Young* remedy. This rule applied even though the statutory remedy in *Seminole Tribe* was an unconstitutional attempt to authorize suit against the state itself.

7. The Court has agreed to decide Couer d'Alene Tribe v. Idaho, 42 F.3d 1244 (9th Cir. 1994), *cert. granted*, 116 S. Ct. 1415 (1996). The court of appeals held that the Tribe could not sue Idaho to quiet title to land, but that it could sue the relevant Idaho officials to enjoin them from regulating the Tribe's use of the land or interfering with its possession.

Page 465. After note 3, add:

On rereading the opinion on remand in Wyatt v. Cole, I realize that the defense it creates is not identical to qualified immunity. Whether the law was clearly settled has at least something to do with it, but the Fifth Circuit opinion is an ill-defined mix of subjective and objective factors, of what defendant actually knew and what he reasonably should have known, of malice and good faith. 994 F.2d at 1120-1121. A more recent Third Circuit opinion puts the emphasis on defendant's subjective good faith; it requires plaintiff to prove at least "gross negligence," and perhaps "recklessness or some higher degree of culpability." Jordan v. Fox,

Rothschild, O'Brien & Frankel, 20 F.3d 1250, 1278 (3d Cir. 1994). Both opinions say they intend to provide more protection to private citizens acting under color of law than *Harlow* provides to public officials. The Ninth Circuit appears to have held that private actors under color of law get no immunity. But the question of reliance on settled law could hardly have arisen; defendants were accused of conspiring with a state judge to fix the outcome of litigation. Kimes v. Stone, 84 F.3d 1121 (9th Cir. 1996).

Page 466. After note 4, add:

4.1. The Court addressed some of these questions in Reynoldsville Casket Co. v. Hyde, 115 S. Ct. 1745 (1995). *Reynoldsville* was a personal injury suit against an out-of-state defendant; plaintiff sued more than two years after the accident, relying on an Ohio statute that tolled the statute of limitations when defendant was not within the state. After she filed suit, the Court struck down the Ohio tolling law as a burden on interstate commerce. Bendix Autolite Corp. v. Midwesco Enterprises, 486 U.S. 888 (1988). So her lawsuit was timely when filed, but barred by limitations after *Bendix*.

Plaintiff cited the Stevens-Souter distinction between retroactivity and remedy, described in note 4. She argued that even though *Bendix* applied retroactively, the Ohio courts had discretion to devise an appropriate remedy for the constitutional violation, and the appropriate remedy could recognize the reliance interests of plaintiffs injured before *Bendix*. No, said the Court. Retroactive application of a new decision requires a retrospective remedy, unless there is some other legal rule, based on something more than mere reliance on the old law, that independently precludes a remedy. For example, taxpayers who paid an illegal tax without protest might be barred by a rule that only those who paid under protest could sue for a refund. The Court said the qualified immunity rules are such an independent rule, based not only on reliance, but on the fear of deterring public officials from doing their duty and the financial burden on the public. Are those independent reasons, or merely the consequences of not protecting reliance?

4.2. Compare Reich v. Collins, 115 S. Ct. 547 (1994). Georgia statutes provided that taxpayers could challenge illegal taxes either before payment, by posting a bond and refusing to pay, or after payment, by suing for a refund. But the supreme court of Georgia held that the refund remedy did not apply to unconstitutional taxes, and that the prepayment remedy was constitutionally sufficient. The Supreme Court of the United States unanimously reversed. Georgia was constitutionally required to provide an adequate remedy. A remedy either before or after payment would suffice, but Georgia could not retroactively eliminate what had appeared on the face of the statute to be a "clear and certain" refund remedy. This appears to be a holding that retroactive application of new decisions is sometimes unconstitutional. No justice in *Reich* bothered to reconcile the holding with any of the earlier opinions, and *Reynoldsville* says nothing about *Reich*. *Reynoldsville* is written in terms of no selective prospectivity, and *Reich* is consistent with that, because the Georgia court's new rule was not applied even to the parties in the first case. But *Reich* would be inconsistent with the rule of universal retroactivity urged by several justices and hinted at in *Harper*.

4.3. *Reich* does make explicit what the earlier tax opinions implied: When the federal Constitution requires state tax refunds, it overrides any state law of sovereign immunity. Id. at 549. But if the state court provides adequate state remedies, it need not provide more complete federal remedies such as attorneys' fees under 42 U.S.C. §§1983 and 1988 (1994). National Private Truck Council v. Oklahoma Tax Commission, 115 S. Ct. 2351 (1995).

4.4. Another variation on retroactivity arose in Ryder v. United States, 115 S. Ct. 2031 (1995). Ryder's conviction in a court-martial was affirmed by a military court that included two judges who had been unconstitutionally appointed by an unauthorized appointing officer. The next higher court also affirmed, invoking the "de facto officer doctrine" to validate official acts taken before the improper appointment was discovered. The Supreme Court reversed, holding that the party who first raises an appointments clause issue is entitled to relief; otherwise, there would be no incentive to raise such issues. The Court distinguished Northern Pipeline Construction Co. v. Marathon Pipe Line Co., 458 U.S. 50 (1982), which had allowed unconstitutionally appointed bankruptcy judges to serve for six months while Congress tried to fix the problem, on the ground that the Court had granted relief to the party before the Court. But isn't *Marathon* inconsistent with the *Harper-Reynoldsville* ban on selective nonretroactivity?

4.5. The Court's insistence on retroactive application of new court decisions is accompanied by a renewed presumption *against* retroactive application of new statutes. Landgraf v. USI Film Products, 114 S. Ct.

1483 (1994); Rivers v. Roadway Express, 114 S. Ct. 1510 (1994). The distinction is largely formal; legislatures make new law, but courts find old law.

This time, the Court defined retroactivity principally in terms of remedies. The Court understood retroactive applications principally in terms of upsetting vested rights or imposing damage liability for acts that were not illegal when committed. The Court agreed, apparently unanimously, that it is not a retroactive application to base prospective relief on a new statute enacted after the events that first led to litigation. *Landgraf*, 114 S. Ct. at 1501; see id. at 1525 (Scalia, J., concurring).

CHAPTER 5

Preventing Harm without Coercion: Declaratory Remedies

A. DECLARATORY JUDGMENTS

Page 483. After note 7, add:

The Federal Circuit recently reported, in an opinion that reflects substantial research, that there is no record of an alleged patent infringer suing to enjoin the patent holder from suing on the patent. In re Lockwood, 50 F.3d 966, 973-974, 979 (Fed. Cir. 1995). The anti-suit injunction was a familiar tool of equity, but for whatever reasons of policy, formalism, or lack of imagination, it was apparently never extended to injunctions against suits for patent infringement.

Page 485. After note 2, add:

2.1. The Supreme Court recently reaffirmed that district courts have broad discretion to decide whether to entertain a declaratory action. Wilton v. Seven Falls Co., 115 S. Ct. 2137 (1995). The language was general, but the context was forum shopping. Plaintiff was an insurance company that had denied coverage and refused to defend in a case that ended in a $100 million judgment against its insured. The insurer sued in federal court for a declaratory judgment that there was no coverage; the insured sued on the policy in state court, joining additional claims and joining nondiverse parties to prevent removal. Even though the federal claim had been filed first, the federal court stayed proceedings in deference to the state court action. It found that the coverage issue could be fairly resolved in the state court action, and that this would avoid piecemeal litigation and prevent forum shopping. The Supreme Court affirmed, deferring to the discretion of the trial court.

Page 495. After the first paragraph of note 3, add:

The Court has emphatically declined to do what I thought it was in the process of doing. "[F]ederal courts have the power to dismiss or remand cases based on abstention principles only where the relief being sought is equitable or otherwise discretionary." Quackenbush v. Allstate Insurance Co., 116 S. Ct. 1712, 1728 (1996). The decision was unanimous, except that Justice Kennedy held open the possibility of exceptional cases. The case involved *Burford* abstention, a doctrine about deference to complex, multiparty, state regulatory proceedings. Burford v. Sun Oil Co., 319 U.S. 315 (1943). But the opinion seems equally applicable to *Younger* and other forms of abstention.

CHAPTER 6

Benefit to Defendant as the Measure of Relief: Restitution

A. THE BASIC PRINCIPLE: PREVENTING UNJUST ENRICHMENT

Page 524. After note 4, add:

Courts are especially reluctant to award restitution (payment for the value of work performed) to attorneys who withdraw from contingent fee contracts without strong justification. For recent examples, see Faro v. Romani, 641 So. 2d 69 (Fla. 1994) (no restitution unless withdrawal required by ethical rules or representation otherwise becomes "legally impossible"); Elliott v. Joyce, 889 P.2d 43 (Colo. 1994) (no restitution unless fee agreement so provides).

C. TRACING DEFENDANT'S BENEFIT: RESTITUTION AND INSOLVENCY

Page 607. After note 7, add:

7.1. The Ninth Circuit has granted a constructive trust of money paid by mistake to the wrong company and then negligently withheld from the company entitled to it. In re Unicom Computer Corp., 13 F.3d 321 (9th Cir. 1994). The court interprets *North American Coin* to mean that the constructive trust claimant must first show a right to constructive trust under state law, and then the bankrupt estate can try to show that enforcement of this trust would be "inequitable as a matter of federal bankruptcy law." Id. at 325.

7.2. The Sixth Circuit has said that "[c]onstructive trusts are anathema to the equities of bankruptcy," and that they will henceforth not be recognized in Sixth Circuit bankruptcies, with the possible exceptions of constructive trusts created by statute or imposed by judicial decree prior to the bankruptcy petition. In re Omegas Group, 16 F.3d 1443, 1451-1452 (6th Cir. 1994).

This sweeping holding appears to have been quite unnecessary to the case, and quite uninformed by the kinds of facts that generate more plausible claims for constructive trust. The constructive trust claimant in *Omegas* was an ordinary contract creditor; the alleged fraud consisted merely of not disclosing the debtor's precarious financial condition; and there was apparently no attempt whatever to identify the res of the trust, which consisted of commingled cash. Thus, there were multiple grounds on which to hold that there was no plausible claim to a constructive trust.

For a strong contrary opinion, see In re Columbia Gas Systems, 997 F.2d 1039 (3d Cir. 1993), enforcing in bankruptcy a constructive trust over money paid to the debtor for the sole purpose of distributing refunds to customers. There was ample room for argument in *Columbia Gas* whether the debtor held the funds as a trustee or simply as a creditor. The majority imposed a trust subject to the tracing rules; the dissenter would have ignored the limitations of the tracing rules and given the customers a full refund.

CHAPTER 7

Punitive Remedies

A. PUNITIVE DAMAGES

1. Common Law and Statutes

Page 671. After note 4, add:

For a new standard out of Texas, see the definition of "gross negligence" in Transportation Insurance Co. v. Moriel, 879 S.W.2d 10 (Tex. 1994), quoted infra at supplement to 702.

Page 672. After note 8, add:

9. Surveys of tort-reform restrictions on punitive damages are proliferating. See BMW, Inc. v. Gore, 116 S. Ct. 1589, 1617-1620 n.6 & app. (1996) (Ginsburg, J., dissenting). She reports thirteen states with statutory caps, thirteen that give a share of punitive awards to the state, twelve with bifurcated trials, and three that have abolished punitives entirely or except where expressly authorized by statute. Twenty-five states appear on at least one of her lists, and this does not include Louisiana, which has never had punitives. See also Thomas Koenig and Michael Rustad, The Quiet Revolution Revisited: An Empirical Study of the Impact of State Tort Reform of Punitive Damages in Products

Liability, 16 Just. Sys. J. 21 (1993) (reporting that twenty-six states require clear and convincing evidence and two states forbid multiple awards for the same products).

10. The Kansas court upheld a statute requiring judges to set the amount of punitives after the jury decides that some punitives should be awarded; the court reasoned that the Kansas right to jury trial does not apply to punitive damages, because plaintiffs had no right to them at common law. Smith v. Printup, 866 P.2d 985, 994-996 (Kan. 1993). Contra, Zoppo v. Homestead Insurance Co., 644 N.E.2d 397, 401-402 (Ohio 1994); see also Henderson v. Alabama Power Co., 627 So. 2d 878 (Ala. 1993), striking down a cap on punitive damages as a violation of the Alabama right to jury trial. It is settled that the federal right to jury trial does not apply in state court.

11. After exhaustive efforts to find punitive damage awards in products liability cases, Koenig and Rustad report that the total of awards is small and declining, with or without tort reform, and that only a small percentage of punitives awarded are collected. Meanwhile, a Texas-only study of punitive damages in all sorts of cases reports enormous increases in both the number and size of awards. J.J. Launie, William P. Jennings, and Robert C. Witt, The Economic Impact of Punitive Damages in Texas (Texas Public Policy Foundation 1994). It is possible that both studies are accurate, but they suggest radically different trends. Neither report gives enough detail to enable readers to identify the sources of disagreement.

2. The Constitution

Page 676. After the first paragraph of note 2, add:

Two more courts have upheld statutes awarding 75 percent of punitive damages to the state. Mack Trucks v. Conkle, 436 S.E.2d 635, 637-640 (Ga. 1993); Shepherd Components v. Brice Petrides-Donohue & Associates, 473 N.W.2d 612, 618-619 (Iowa 1991). The Georgia statute applies only to products liability actions, and it provides that there can be only one award of punitive damages against a defendant for the same defective product. The court reasoned that a mass-produced product endangers the whole public, and that the lucky first plaintiff should share the single award of punitive damages with the public. Similar reasoning appears to underlie the Iowa statute, which does not apply if the jury finds on a special interrogatory that defendant's wrongful conduct was aimed specifically at the plaintiff.

Page 677. Replace note 6 and *TXO* with the following:

6. The Court finally reversed an award of punitive damages in Honda Motor Co. v. Oberg, 114 S. Ct. 2331 (1994). *Honda* involved an apparently unique provision of the Oregon Constitution, which entirely precluded judicial review of the amount of a damage award. The Court reviewed the power of common law judges to set aside excessive verdicts, and held that this power was an essential component of procedural due process.

Justice Ginsburg, joined by Chief Justice Rehnquist, dissented. She thought the power to set aside excessive verdicts was rarely exercised at common law, and that considered as a whole, Oregon exercised more control over juries than common law judges at the time of the founding.

On remand, the Oregon court decided that the constitutionally required standard of review is whether the verdict was "within the range that a rational juror would be entitled to award in the light of the record as a whole." 888 P.2d 8, 12 (Or. 1995). Would that constitutional standard add anything to state law review for excessiveness in the states that have such review? Applying that standard, the Oregon court affirmed the original verdict of $5 million in punitive damages. Honda had designed and sold an all-terrain vehicle that rolled over and injured plaintiff; the court cited evidence that Honda had sold the vehicles for fifteen years after it knew of the danger, and that its net worth at the time of trial was $4.9 billion.

BMW, INC. v. GORE

116 S. Ct. 1589 (1996)

JUSTICE STEVENS delivered the opinion of the Court. . . .

I

In January 1990, Dr. Ira Gore, Jr. . . . purchased a black BMW sports sedan for $40,750.88 . . . After driving the car for approximately nine months, and without noticing any flaws in its appearance, Dr. Gore took the car to "Slick Finish" . . . to make it look "'snazzier than it normally would appear.'" 646 So. 2d 619, 621 (Ala. 1994). Mr. Slick, the proprietor, detected evidence that the car had been repainted.[1] . . .

BMW acknowledged that it had adopted a nationwide policy in 1983 concerning cars that were damaged in the course of manufacture or transportation. If the cost of repairing the damage exceeded 3 percent of the car's suggested retail price, the car was placed in company service for a period of time and then sold as used. If the repair cost did not exceed 3 percent of the suggested retail price, however, the car was sold as new without advising the dealer that any repairs had been made. Because the $601.37 cost of repainting Dr. Gore's car was only about 1.5 percent of its suggested retail price, BMW did not disclose the damage or repair . . .

Dr. Gore asserted that his repainted car was worth less than a car that had not been refinished. To prove his actual damages of $4,000, he relied on the testimony of a former BMW dealer, who estimated that the value of a repainted BMW was approximately 10 percent less than the value of a new car that had not been damaged and repaired. To support his claim for punitive damages, Dr. Gore introduced evidence that since 1983 BMW had sold 983 refinished cars as new, including 14 in Alabama, without disclosing that the cars had been repainted before sale at a cost of more than $300 per vehicle. Using the actual damage estimate of $4,000 per vehicle, Dr. Gore argued that a punitive award of $4 million would provide an appropriate penalty for selling approximately 1,000 cars for more than they were worth. . . .

BMW argued that it was under no obligation to disclose repairs of minor damage to new cars and that Dr. Gore's car was as good as a car with the original factory finish. It disputed Dr. Gore's assertion that the value of the car was impaired by the repainting and argued that this good-faith belief made a punitive award inappropriate. . . .

The jury returned a verdict finding BMW liable for compensatory damages of $4,000. In addition, the jury assessed $4 million in punitive damages, based on a determination that the nondisclosure policy constituted "gross, oppressive or malicious" fraud. See Ala. Code §§6-11-20, 6-11-21 (1993).

1. . . . The parties presumed that the damage was caused by exposure to acid rain during transit between the manufacturing plant in Germany and the preparation center.

[On a post-trial motion], BMW . . . introduced evidence to establish that its nondisclosure policy was consistent with the laws of roughly 25 States defining the disclosure obligations of automobile manufacturers, distributors, and dealers. The most stringent of these statutes required disclosure of repairs costing more than 3 percent of the suggested retail price; none mandated disclosure of less costly repairs.[7] . . .

BMW also drew the court's attention to the fact that its nondisclosure policy had never been adjudged unlawful before this action was filed. Just months before Dr. Gore's case went to trial, the jury in a similar lawsuit filed by another Alabama BMW purchaser found that BMW's failure to disclose paint repair constituted fraud. Yates v. BMW, Inc., 642 So. 2d 937 (Ala. 1993).[8] . . . When the $4 million verdict was returned in this case, BMW promptly instituted a nationwide policy of full disclosure of all repairs, no matter how minor. . . .

Dr. Gore asserted that the policy change demonstrated the efficacy of the punitive damages award. He noted that . . . BMW had received a number of customer complaints relating to undisclosed repairs and had settled some lawsuits. . . .

The trial judge denied BMW's post-trial motion, holding . . . that the award was not excessive. On appeal, the Alabama Supreme Court also rejected BMW's claim that the award exceeded the constitutionally permissible amount. 646 So. 2d 619 (1994). The court's excessiveness inquiry applied the factors articulated in Green Oil Co. v. Hornsby, 539 So. 2d 218, 223-224 (Ala. 1989), and approved in Pacific Mutual Life Insurance Co. v. Haslip, 499 U.S. 1, 21-22 (1991). 646 So. 2d at 624-625. Based on its analysis, the court concluded that BMW's conduct was "reprehensible"; the nondisclosure was profitable for the company; the judgment "would not have a substantial impact upon [BMW's] financial position"; the litigation had been expensive; no criminal sanctions had been imposed on BMW for the same conduct; the award of *no* punitive damages in *Yates* reflected "the inherent uncertainty of the

7. . . . [A] Georgia statute enacted after Dr. Gore purchased his car would require disclosure of similar repairs to a car before it was sold in Georgia. Ga. Code Ann. §40-1-5(b)-(e) (1994).

8. While awarding a comparable amount of compensatory damages, the *Yates* jury awarded no punitive damages at all. . . . [I]nstead of offering evidence of 983 repairs costing more than $300 each, [Yates] . . . show[ed] that [BMW] had sold over 5,800 new BMW vehicles without disclosing that they had been repaired.

trial process"; and the punitive award bore a "reasonable relationship" to "the harm that was likely to occur from [BMW's] conduct as well as . . . the harm that actually occurred." Id. at 625-627.

The Alabama Supreme Court did, however, rule in BMW's favor on one critical point: The court found that the jury improperly computed the amount of punitive damages by multiplying Dr. Gore's compensatory damages by the number of similar sales in other jurisdictions. Id. at 627. Having found the verdict tainted, the court held that "a constitutionally reasonable punitive damages award in this case is $2,000,000," id. at 629, and therefore ordered a remittitur in that amount. The court's discussion of the amount of its remitted award expressly disclaimed any reliance on "acts that occurred in other jurisdictions" . . .

II

Punitive damages may properly be imposed to further a State's legitimate interests in punishing unlawful conduct and deterring its repetition. In our federal system, States necessarily have considerable flexibility in determining the level of punitive damages that they will allow in different classes of cases and in any particular case. Most States that authorize exemplary damages afford the jury similar latitude, requiring only that the damages awarded be reasonably necessary to vindicate the State's legitimate interests in punishment and deterrence. Only when an award can fairly be categorized as "grossly excessive" in relation to these interests does it enter the zone of arbitrariness that violates the Due Process Clause of the Fourteenth Amendment. Cf. TXO Production Corp. v. Alliance Resources Corp., 509 U.S. 443, 456 (1993) (plurality opinion). . . .

No one doubts that a State may protect its citizens by prohibiting deceptive trade practices and by requiring automobile distributors to disclose presale repairs that affect the value of a new car. But the States need not, and in fact do not, provide such protection in a uniform manner. . . . The result is a patchwork of rules representing the diverse policy judgments of lawmakers in 50 States.

That diversity demonstrates that reasonable people may disagree about the value of a full disclosure requirement. Some legislatures may conclude that affirmative disclosure requirements are unnecessary . . . Those legislatures that do adopt affirmative disclosure obligations may take into account the cost of government regulation, choosing to draw a line exempting minor repairs from such a requirement. . . .[14] . . .

We think it follows from . . . principles of state sovereignty and comity that a State may not impose economic sanctions on violators of its laws with the intent of changing the tortfeasors' lawful conduct in other States. Before this Court Dr. Gore argued that the large punitive damages award was necessary to induce BMW to change the nationwide policy that it adopted in 1983. But by attempting to alter BMW's nationwide policy, Alabama would be infringing on the policy choices of other States. To avoid such encroachment, the economic penalties that a State such as Alabama inflicts on those who transgress its laws . . . must be supported by the State's interest in protecting its own consumers and its own economy. . . .

[N]either the jury nor the trial court was presented with evidence that any of BMW's out-of-state conduct was unlawful. . . .[20] The Alabama Supreme Court therefore properly . . . based its remitted award solely on conduct that occurred within Alabama.[21] . . .

III

Elementary notions of fairness enshrined in our constitutional jurisprudence dictate that a person receive fair notice not only of the conduct that will subject him to punishment but also of the severity of the penalty that a State may impose. Three guideposts, each of which indicates that BMW did not receive adequate notice of the magnitude of the sanction that Alabama might impose for adhering to the nondisclosure policy adopted

14. Also, a state legislature might plausibly conclude that the . . . costs associated with full disclosure would [raise] car prices to the State's residents.

20. Given that the verdict was based in part on out-of-state conduct that was lawful where it occurred, we need not consider whether one State may properly attempt to change a tortfeasors' *unlawful* conduct in another State.

21. Of course, the fact that the Alabama Supreme Court correctly concluded that it was error for the jury to use the number of sales in other States as a multiplier in computing the amount of its punitive sanction does not mean that evidence describing out-of-state transactions is irrelevant in a case of this kind. To the contrary, as we stated in *TXO*, 509 U.S. at 462 n.28 (plurality opinion) . . . , such evidence is relevant to the determination of the degree of reprehensibility of the defendant's conduct.

in 1983, lead us to the conclusion that the $2 million award against BMW is grossly excessive . . .

Degree of Reprehensibility

Perhaps the most important indicium of the reasonableness of a punitive damages award is the degree of reprehensibility of the defendant's conduct. . . . This principle reflects the accepted view that some wrongs are more blameworthy than others. Thus, . . . "nonviolent crimes are less serious than crimes marked by violence or the threat of violence." Solem v. Helm, 463 U.S. 277, 292-293 (1983). . . . "[T]rickery and deceit," *TXO*, 509 U.S. at 462 (plurality opinion), are more reprehensible than negligence. . . .

In this case, none of the aggravating factors associated with particularly reprehensible conduct is present. The harm BMW inflicted on Dr. Gore was purely economic in nature. The presale refinishing of the car had no effect on its performance or safety features, or even its appearance for at least nine months after his purchase. BMW's conduct evinced no indifference to or reckless disregard for the health and safety of others. To be sure, infliction of economic injury, especially when done intentionally through affirmative acts of misconduct, or when the target is financially vulnerable, can warrant a substantial penalty. But this observation does not convert all acts that cause economic harm into torts that are sufficiently reprehensible to justify a significant sanction in addition to compensatory damages.

Dr. Gore contends that BMW's conduct was particularly reprehensible because nondisclosure of the repairs to his car formed part of a nationwide pattern of tortious conduct. Certainly, evidence that a defendant has repeatedly engaged in prohibited conduct while knowing or suspecting that it was unlawful would provide relevant support for an argument that strong medicine is required to cure the defendant's disrespect for the law. . . .

In support of his thesis, Dr. Gore advances two arguments. First, he asserts that the state disclosure statutes supplement, rather than supplant, existing remedies for breach of contract and common-law fraud. Thus, according to Dr. Gore, the statutes may not properly be viewed as immunizing from liability the nondisclosure of repairs costing less than the applicable statutory threshold. . . .

[O]nly state courts may authoritatively construe state statutes. . . .[27] A review of the text of the statutes, however, persuades us that in the absence of a state-court determination to the contrary, a corporate executive could reasonably interpret the disclosure requirements as establishing safe harbors. . . . [T]he record contains no evidence that BMW's decision to follow a disclosure policy that coincided with the strictest extant state statute was sufficiently reprehensible to justify a $2 million award of punitive damages.

Dr. Gore's second argument for treating BMW as a recidivist is that the company should have anticipated that its actions would be considered fraudulent in some, if not all, jurisdictions. This contention overlooks the fact that actionable fraud requires a *material* misrepresentation or omission. This qualifier invites line drawing of just the sort engaged in by States with disclosure statutes and by BMW. We do not think it can be disputed that there may exist minor imperfections in the finish of a new car that can be repaired (or indeed, left unrepaired) without materially affecting the car's value. There is no evidence that BMW acted in bad faith when it sought to establish the appropriate line between presumptively minor damage and damage requiring disclosure to purchasers. For this purpose, BMW could reasonably rely on state disclosure statutes for guidance. . . . [T]here is no evidence that BMW persisted in a course of conduct after it had been adjudged unlawful on even one occasion, let alone repeated occasions.

Finally, the record in this case discloses no deliberate false statements, acts of affirmative misconduct, or concealment of evidence of improper motive, such as were present in *Haslip* and *TXO*. We accept, of course, the jury's finding that BMW suppressed a material fact which Alabama law obligated it to communicate to prospective purchasers of repainted cars in that State. But the omission of a material fact may be less

27. In Jeter v. M & M Dodge, 634 So. 2d 1383 (La. App. 1994), a Louisiana court of appeals suggested that the Louisiana disclosure statute functions as a safe harbor. . . . During the pendency of this litigation, Alabama enacted a disclosure statute which defines "material" damage to a new car as damage requiring repairs costing in excess of 3 percent of suggested retail price or $500, whichever is greater. Ala. Code §8-19-5(22) (1993). After its decision in this case, the Alabama Supreme Court stated in dicta that the remedies available under this section . . . did not displace or alter pre-existing remedies available under either the common law or other statutes. Hines v. Riverside Chevrolet-Olds, 655 So. 2d 909, 917 n.2 (Ala. 1994). . . .

reprehensible than a deliberate false statement, particularly when there is a good-faith basis for believing that no duty to disclose exists.

That conduct is sufficiently reprehensible to give rise to tort liability, and even a modest award of exemplary damages, does not establish the high degree of culpability that warrants a substantial punitive damages award. Because this case exhibits none of the circumstances ordinarily associated with egregiously improper conduct, we are persuaded that BMW's conduct was not sufficiently reprehensible to warrant imposition of a $2 million exemplary damages award.

Ratio

The second and perhaps most commonly cited indicium of an unreasonable or excessive punitive damages award is its ratio to the actual harm inflicted on the plaintiff. . . .

In *Haslip* we concluded that even though a punitive damages award of "more than 4 times the amount of compensatory damages," might be "close to the line," it did not "cross the line into the area of constitutional impropriety." *Haslip*, 499 U.S. at 23-24. *TXO* refined this analysis by confirming that the proper inquiry is "'whether there is a reasonable relationship between the punitive damages award and *the harm likely to result* from the defendant's conduct as well as the harm that actually has occurred.'" *TXO*, 509 U.S. at 460 (plurality opinion), quoting *Haslip*, 499 U.S. at 21. Thus, in upholding the $10 million award in *TXO*, we relied on the difference between that figure and the harm to the victim that would have ensued if the tortious plan had succeeded. That difference suggested that the relevant ratio was not more than 10 to 1.

The $2 million in punitive damages awarded to Dr. Gore by the Alabama Supreme Court is 500 times the amount of his actual harm as determined by the jury.[35] Moreover, there is no suggestion that Dr. Gore or any other BMW purchaser was threatened with any additional potential harm by BMW's nondisclosure policy. The disparity in this case is thus dramatically greater than those considered in *Haslip* and *TXO*.

35. Even assuming each repainted BMW suffers a diminution in value of approximately $4,000, the award is 35 times greater than the total damages of all 14 Alabama consumers who purchased repainted BMW's.

Of course, we have consistently rejected the notion that the constitutional line is marked by a simple mathematical formula, even one that compares actual *and potential* damages to the punitive award. *TXO*, 509 U.S. at 458 (plurality opinion). Indeed, low awards of compensatory damages may properly support a higher ratio than high compensatory awards, if, for example, a particularly egregious act has resulted in only a small amount of economic damages. A higher ratio may also be justified in cases in which the injury is hard to detect or the monetary value of noneconomic harm might have been difficult to determine. It is appropriate, therefore, to reiterate our rejection of a categorical approach. Once again, "we return to what we said . . . in *Haslip*: 'We need not, and indeed we cannot, draw a mathematical bright line between the constitutionally acceptable and the constitutionally unacceptable that would fit every case. We can say, however, that [a] general concer[n] of reasonableness . . . properly enter[s] into the constitutional calculus.'" *TXO*, 509 U.S. at 458 (plurality opinion) (quoting *Haslip*, 499 U.S. at 18). In most cases, the ratio will be within a constitutionally acceptable range, and remittitur will not be justified on this basis. When the ratio is a breathtaking 500 to 1, however, the award must surely "raise a suspicious judicial eyebrow." *TXO*, 509 U.S. at 482 (O'Connor, J., dissenting).

Sanctions for Comparable Misconduct

Comparing the punitive damages award and the civil or criminal penalties that could be imposed for comparable misconduct provides a third indicium of excessiveness. . . . In *Haslip*, 499 U.S. at 23, the Court noted that although the exemplary award was "much in excess of the fine that could be imposed," imprisonment was also authorized in the criminal context. In this case the $2 million economic sanction imposed on BMW is substantially greater than the statutory fines available in Alabama and elsewhere for similar malfeasance.

The maximum civil penalty authorized by the Alabama Legislature for a violation of its Deceptive Trade Practices Act is $2,000; other States authorize more severe sanctions, with the maxima ranging from $5,000 to $10,000. Significantly, some statutes draw a distinction between first offenders and recidivists; thus, in New York the penalty is $50 for a first offense and $250 for subsequent offenses. None of these statutes would provide an out-of-state distributor with fair notice that the first violation—or, indeed the first 14 violations—of its provisions might subject an offender to a multimillion dollar penalty. . . .

The sanction imposed in this case cannot be justified on the ground that it was necessary to deter future misconduct without considering whether less drastic remedies could be expected to achieve that goal. The fact that a multimillion dollar penalty prompted a change in policy sheds no light on the question whether a lesser deterrent would have adequately protected the interests of Alabama consumers. . . .

IV

We assume . . . that the undisclosed damage to the new BMWs affected their actual value. . . . [W]e also assume that [BMW] knew, or should have known, that as time passed the repainted cars would lose their attractive appearance more rapidly than other BMWs. Moreover, we of course accept the Alabama courts' view that the state interest in protecting its citizens from deceptive trade practices justifies a sanction in addition to the recovery of compensatory damages. We cannot, however, accept the conclusion . . . that BMW's conduct was sufficiently egregious to justify a punitive sanction that is tantamount to a severe criminal penalty.

The fact that BMW is a large corporation rather than an impecunious individual does not diminish its entitlement to fair notice of the demands that the several States impose on the conduct of its business. Indeed, its status as an active participant in the national economy implicates the federal interest in preventing individual States from imposing undue burdens on interstate commerce. . . .

Whether the appropriate remedy requires a new trial or merely an independent determination by the Alabama Supreme Court of the award necessary to vindicate the economic interests of Alabama consumers is a matter that should be addressed by the state court in the first instance.

The judgment is reversed, and the case is remanded for further proceedings not inconsistent with this opinion. . . .

JUSTICE BREYER, with whom JUSTICES O'CONNOR and SOUTER join, concurring. . . .

The Court's opinion, which I join, explains why we have concluded that this award, in this case, was "grossly excessive" in relation to legitimate punitive damages objectives, and hence an arbitrary deprivation of life, liberty, or property in violation of the Due Process Clause. Members of this Court have generally thought, however, that if "fair procedures were followed, a judgment that is a product of that process is entitled to a strong presumption of validity." *TXO*, 509 U.S. at 457 (plurality opinion). And the Court also has found that punitive damages procedures very similar to those followed here were not, by themselves, fundamentally unfair. *Haslip*, 499 U.S. at 15-24. Thus, I believe it important to explain why this presumption of validity is overcome in this instance.

The reason flows from the Court's emphasis in *Haslip* upon the constitutional importance of legal standards that provide "reasonable constraints" within which "discretion is exercised," that assure "meaningful and adequate review by the trial court whenever a jury has fixed the punitive damages," and permit "appellate review [that] makes certain that the punitive damages are reasonable in their amount and rational in light of their purpose to punish what has occurred and to deter its repetition." Id. at 20-21.

This constitutional concern, itself harkening back to the Magna Carta, arises out of the basic unfairness of depriving citizens of life, liberty, or property, through the application, not of law and legal processes, but of arbitrary coercion. Requiring the application of law, rather than a decisionmaker's caprice, . . . also helps to assure the uniform general treatment of similarly situated persons that is the essence of law itself.

Legal standards need not be precise in order to satisfy this constitutional concern. See *Haslip*, 499 U.S. at 20 (comparing punitive damages standards to such legal standards as "reasonable care," "due diligence," and "best interests of the child"). But they must offer some kind of constraint upon a jury or court's discretion, and thus protection against purely arbitrary behavior. The standards the Alabama courts applied here are vague and open-ended to the point where they risk arbitrary results. In my view, although the vagueness of those standards does not, by itself, violate due process, see *Haslip*, it does invite the kind of scrutiny the Court has given the particular verdict before us. . . .

First, the Alabama statute that permits punitive damages does not itself contain a standard that readily distinguishes between conduct warranting very small, and conduct warranting very large, punitive damages awards. That statute permits punitive damages in cases of "oppression, fraud, wantonness, or malice." Ala. Code §6-11-20(a) (1993). But the statute goes on to define those terms broadly, to encompass far more than the egregious conduct that those terms, at first reading, might seem to imply. . . .

Second, the Alabama courts, in this case, have applied the "factors" intended to constrain punitive damages awards, in a way that belies that purpose. Green Oil Co. v. Hornsby, 539 So. 2d 218 (Ala. 1989), sets forth seven factors that appellate courts use to determine whether . . . a jury award was "grossly excessive," id. at 223, and which, in principle, might make up for the lack of significant constraint in the statute. But, as the Alabama courts have authoritatively interpreted them, . . . they impose little actual constraint.

(a) *Green Oil* requires that a punitive damages award "bear a reasonable relationship to the harm that is likely to occur from the defendant's conduct as well as to the harm that actually has occurred." But . . . [t]o find a "reasonable relationship" between purely economic harm totaling $56,000, without significant evidence of future repetition, and a punitive award of $2 million is to empty the "reasonable relationship" test of meaningful content. As thus construed, it does not set forth a legal standard that could have significantly constrained the discretion of Alabama factfinders.

(b) *Green Oil*'s second factor is the "degree of reprehensibility" of the defendant's conduct. . . . I do not see how the Alabama courts could find conduct that (they assumed) caused $56,000 of relevant economic harm *especially* or *unusually* reprehensible enough to warrant $2 million in punitive damages . . . To find to the contrary . . . is not simply unreasonable; it is to make "reprehensibility" a concept without constraining force . . .

(c) *Green Oil*'s third factor requires "punitive damages" to "remove the profit" of the illegal activity and "be in excess of the profit, so that the defendant recognizes a loss." This factor has the ability to limit awards to a fixed, rational amount. But as applied, that concept's potential was not realized, for the court did not limit the award to anywhere near the $56,000 in profits evidenced in the record. . . .

(d) *Green Oil*'s fourth factor is the "financial position" of the defendant. Since a fixed dollar award will punish a poor person more than a wealthy one, one can understand the relevance of this factor to the state's interest in retribution (though not necessarily to its interest in deterrence, given the more distant relation between a defendant's wealth and its responses to economic incentives). This factor, however, is not necessarily intended to act as a significant constraint on punitive awards.

Rather, it provides an open-ended basis for inflating awards when the defendant is wealthy . . . That does not make its use unlawful or inappropriate; it simply means that this factor cannot make up for the failure of other factors . . .

(e) *Green Oil*'s fifth factor is the "costs of litigation" and the State's desire "to encourage plaintiffs to bring wrongdoers to trial." This standard provides meaningful constraint to the extent that the enhancement it authorized is linked to a fixed, ascertainable amount approximating actual costs, even when defined generously to reflect the contingent nature of plaintiffs' victories. But as this case shows, the factor cannot operate as a constraint when an award much in excess of costs is approved for other reasons. . . .

(f) *Green Oil*'s sixth factor is whether . . . "criminal sanctions have been imposed on the defendant for his conduct." This factor did not apply here.

(g) *Green Oil*'s seventh factor requires that "other civil actions" filed "against the same defendant, based on the same conduct" be considered in mitigation. That factor did not apply here. . . .

Third, the state courts . . . referred to [no] other standard that . . . might have supplied the constraining legal force that the statute and *Green Oil* standards (as interpreted here) lack. Dr. Gore did argue to the jury an economic theory based on the need to offset the totality of the harm that the defendant's conduct caused. Some theory of that general kind might have provided a significant constraint on arbitrary awards (at least where confined to the relevant harm-causing conduct). Some economists, for example, have argued for a standard that would deter illegal activity causing solely economic harm through the use of punitive damages awards that, as a whole, would take from a wrongdoer the total cost of the harm caused. . . . My understanding of the intuitive essence of some of those theories . . . is that they could permit juries to calculate punitive damages by making a rough estimate of global harm, dividing that estimate by a similarly rough estimate of the number of successful lawsuits that would likely be brought, and adding generous attorneys fees and other costs. Smaller damages would not sufficiently discourage firms from engaging in the harmful conduct, while larger damages would "over-deter" by leading potential defendants to spend more to prevent the activity that causes the economic harm, say, through employee training, than the cost of the harm itself. Larger damages might also "double count" by including in the punitive damages award some of the compensatory, or punitive, damages that subsequent plaintiffs would also recover.

The record before us, however, contains nothing suggesting that the Alabama Supreme Court, when determining the allowable award, applied *any* "economic" theory that might explain the $2 million recovery. And courts properly tend to judge the rationality of judicial actions in terms of the reasons that were given, and the facts that were before the court, not those that might have been given on the basis of some conceivable set of facts . . .

Fourth, I cannot find any community understanding or historic practice that this award might exemplify and which, therefore, would provide background standards constraining arbitrary behavior and excessive awards. A punitive damages award of $2 million for intentional misrepresentation causing $56,000 of harm is extraordinary by historical standards, and, as far as I am aware, finds no analogue until relatively recent times. . . .

Fifth, there are no other legislative enactments here that classify awards and impose quantitative limits that would significantly cabin the fairly unbounded discretion created by the absence of constraining legal standards.

The upshot is that the rules that purport to channel discretion in this kind of case, here did not do so in fact. That means that the award in this case was both (a) the product of a system of standards that did not significantly constrain a court's, and hence a jury's, discretion in making that award; and (b) was grossly excessive in light of the State's legitimate punitive damages objectives.

The first of these reasons has special importance where courts review a jury-determined punitive damages award. That is because one cannot expect to direct jurors like legislators through the ballot box; nor can one expect those jurors to interpret law like judges, who work within a discipline and hierarchical organization that normally promotes roughly uniform interpretation and application of the law. Yet here Alabama expects jurors to act, at least a little, like legislators or judges, for it permits them, to a certain extent, to create public policy and to apply that policy, not to compensate a victim, but to achieve a policy-related objective outside the confines of the particular case. . . .

The second reason—the severe disproportionality between the award and the legitimate punitive damages objectives—reflects a judgment about a matter of degree. . . . Yet whatever the difficulties of drawing a precise line, . . . it is not difficult to say that this award lies on the line's far side. . . .

These two reasons taken together overcome what would otherwise amount to a "strong presumption of validity." *TXO*, 509 U.S. at 457 (plurality opinion). And, for those two reasons, I conclude that the award in this unusual case violates the basic guarantee of nonarbitrary governmental behavior that the Due Process Clause provides.

JUSTICE SCALIA, with whom JUSTICE THOMAS joins, dissenting.

Today we see the latest manifestation of this Court's recent and increasingly insistent "concern about punitive damages that 'run wild.'" *Haslip*, 499 U.S. at 18. Since the Constitution does not make that concern any of our business, the Court's activities in this area are an unjustified incursion into the province of state governments. . . .

[A] state trial procedure that commits the decision whether to impose punitive damages, and the amount, to the discretion of the jury, subject to some judicial review for "reasonableness," furnishes a defendant with all the process that is "due." . . . What the Fourteenth Amendment's procedural guarantee assures is an opportunity to contest the reasonableness of a damages judgment in state court; but there is no federal guarantee a damages award actually *be* reasonable.

This view, which adheres to the text of the Due Process Clause, has not prevailed in our punitive-damages cases. When, however, a constitutional doctrine adopted by the Court is not only mistaken but also insusceptible of principled application, I do not feel bound to give it stare decisis effect—indeed, I do not feel justified in doing so. . . .

I

The most significant aspects of today's decision—the identification of a "substantive due process" right against a "grossly excessive" award, and the concomitant assumption of ultimate authority to decide anew a matter of "reasonableness" resolved in lower court proceedings—are of course not new. *Haslip* and *TXO* revived the notion, moribund since its appearance in the first years of this century, that the measure of civil punishment poses a question of constitutional dimension to be answered by this Court. Neither of those cases, however, nor any of the precedents upon which they relied, actually took the step of declaring a punitive award unconstitutional simply because it was "too big."

At the time of adoption of the Fourteenth Amendment, it was well understood that punitive damages represent the assessment by the jury, as the voice of the community, of the measure of punishment the defendant deserved. Today's decision, though dressed up as a legal opinion, is really no more than a disagreement with the community's sense of indignation or outrage expressed in the punitive award of the Alabama jury, as reduced by the State Supreme Court. . . .

II

One might understand the Court's eagerness to enter this field, rather than leave it with the state legislatures, if it had something useful to say. In fact, however, its opinion provides virtually no guidance . . . as to what a "constitutionally proper" level of punitive damages might be. . . .

"Alabama does not have the power," the Court says, "to punish BMW for conduct that was lawful where it occurred and that had no impact on Alabama or its residents." That may be true, though only in the narrow sense that a person cannot be *held liable to be punished* on the basis of a lawful act. But if a person has been held subject to punishment because he committed an unlawful act, the *degree* of his punishment assuredly can be increased on the basis of any other conduct of his that displays his wickedness, unlawful or not. Criminal sentences can be computed, we have said, on the basis of "information concerning every aspect of a defendant's life," Williams v. New York, 337 U.S. 241, 250-252 (1949). . . . Why could the Supreme Court of Alabama not consider lawful (but disreputable) conduct, both inside and outside Alabama, for the purpose of assessing just how bad an actor BMW was? . . .

[T]he Alabama Supreme Court—whether it was constitutionally required to or not—"expressly disclaimed any reliance on acts that occurred in other jurisdictions." . . . The Court's sweeping (and largely unsupported) statements regarding the relationship of punitive awards to lawful or unlawful out-of-state conduct are the purest dicta.

III . . .

[T]he Court identifies "[t]hree guideposts" that lead it to the conclusion that the award in this case is excessive . . . Apparently (though it is by no means clear) all three federal "guideposts" can be overridden if "necessary to deter future misconduct," a loophole that will encourage state reviewing courts to uphold awards as necessary for the "adequat[e] protect[ion]" of state consumers. By effectively requiring state reviewing courts to concoct rationalizations—whether within the "guideposts" or through the loophole—to justify the intuitive punitive reactions of state juries, the Court accords neither category of institution the respect it deserves. . . .

In truth, the "guideposts" mark a road to nowhere; they provide no real guidance at all. As to "degree of reprehensibility" of the defendant's conduct, we learn that "'nonviolent crimes are less serious than crimes marked by violence or the threat of violence,'" (quoting Solem v. Helm, 463 U.S. 277, 292-293 (1983)), and that "'trickery and deceit'" are "more reprehensible than negligence." As to the ratio of punitive to compensatory damages, we are told that a "'general concer[n] of reasonableness . . . enter[s] into the constitutional calculus,'" (quoting *TXO*, 509 U.S. at 458 (plurality opinion))—though even "a breathtaking 500 to 1" will not necessarily do anything more than "'raise a suspicious judicial eyebrow,'" (quoting *TXO*, 509 U.S. at 481 (O'Connor, J., dissenting), an opinion which, when confronted with that "breathtaking" ratio, approved it). And as to legislative sanctions provided for comparable misconduct, they should be accorded "'substantial deference,'" (quoting Browning-Ferris Industries v. Kelco Disposal, 492 U.S. 257, 301 (1989) (O'Connor, J., dissenting in part)). . . .

These criss-crossing platitudes yield no real answers in . . . real cases. . . . [T]he Court nowhere says that these three "guideposts" are the only guideposts; indeed, it makes very clear that they are not—explaining away the earlier opinions that do not really follow these "guideposts" on the basis of *additional* factors, thereby "reiterat[ing] our rejection of a categorical approach." In other words, even these utter platitudes, if they should ever happen to produce an answer, may be overridden by other unnamed considerations. The Court has constructed a framework that does not genuinely constrain, that does not inform state legislatures and lower courts—that does nothing at all except confer an artificial air of doctrinal analysis upon its essentially ad hoc determination that this particular award of punitive damages was not "fair." . . .

The relationship between judicial application of the new "guideposts" and jury findings poses a real problem for the Court, since as a matter of logic there is no more justification for ignoring the jury's determination as to *how* reprehensible petitioner's conduct was (i.e., how much it deserves to be punished), than there is for ignoring its determination that it was reprehensible *at all* (i.e., that the wrong was willful and punitive damages are therefore recoverable). That the issue has been framed in terms of a constitutional right against unreasonably *excessive* awards should not obscure the fact that the logical and necessary consequence of the Court's approach is the recognition of a constitutional right against unreasonably *imposed* awards as well. The elevation of "fairness" in punishment to a principle of "substantive due process" means that every punitive award unreasonably imposed is unconstitutional; such an award is by definition excessive, since it attaches a penalty to conduct undeserving of punishment. . . .

For the foregoing reasons, I respectfully dissent.

JUSTICE GINSBURG, with whom CHIEF JUSTICE REHNQUIST joins, dissenting. . . .

I

The respect due the Alabama Supreme Court requires that we strip from this case a false issue: no impermissible "extraterritoriality" infects the judgment before us; the excessiveness of the award is the sole issue genuinely presented. . . .

Sales nationwide, Alabama's Supreme Court said, were admissible "as to the issue of a 'pattern and practice' of such acts." Id. at 627. There was "no error," the court reiterated, "in the admission of the evidence that showed how pervasive the nondisclosure policy was and the intent behind [BMW's] adoption of it." Id. at 628. . . . See *TXO*, 509 U.S. at 462 & n.28 (plurality opinion) (characterizing as "well-settled" the admissibility of "evidence of [defendant's] alleged wrongdoing in other parts of the country" and of defendant's "wealth").

Alabama's highest court next declared that the

> jury could not use the number of similar acts that a defendant has committed in other jurisdictions as a multiplier when determining the *dollar amount* of a punitive damages award . . . because neither the jury nor the trial court had evidence before it showing in which states the conduct was wrongful.

646 So.2d at 627. . . .

Because the jury apparently (and erroneously) had used acts in other states as a multiplier to arrive at a $4 million sum for punitive damages, the Alabama Supreme Court itself determined "'the maximum amount that a properly functioning jury could have awarded.'" 646 So. 2d at 630 (Houston, J., concurring) (quoting Big B v. Cottingham, 634 So. 2d 999, 1006 (Ala. 1993)). . . . As this Court recognizes, the Alabama high court "properly eschewed reliance on BMW's out-of-state conduct and based its remitted award solely on conduct that occurred within Alabama."

II . . .

B

The Court finds Alabama's $2 million award not simply excessive, but grossly so, and therefore unconstitutional. The decision leads us further into territory traditionally within the States' domain, and commits the Court, now and again, to correct "misapplication of a properly stated rule of law." But cf. S. Ct. Rule 10 ("A petition for a writ of certiorari is rarely granted when the asserted error consists of erroneous factual findings or the misapplication of a properly stated rule of law."). The Court is not well equipped for this mission. Tellingly, the Court repeats that it brings to the task no "mathematical formula," no "categorical approach," no "bright line." It has only a vague concept of substantive due process, a "raised eyebrow" test, as its ultimate guide.

In contrast to habeas corpus review under 28 U.S.C. §2254, the Court will work at this business alone. It will not be aided by the federal district courts and courts of appeals. . . . And the reexamination prominent in state courts and in legislative arenas serves to underscore why the Court's enterprise is undue.

For the reasons stated, I dissent from this Court's disturbance of the judgment the Alabama Supreme Court has made.

Page 691. Before note 1, add:

0.1. The notes that follow were written with reference to TXO Production Corp. v. Alliance Resources Corp., 509 U.S. 443 (1993), reprinted in the main volume at 677 and frequently quoted in *BMW*. The questions raised in the notes are equally applicable to both cases.

TXO purchased mineral rights from Alliance, promising royalties that were likely to run to millions of dollars—Alliance claimed five to eight million, but that was disputed. Then TXO paid $6,000 to buy the same rights from a third party, and tried to renegotiate or renege on the Alliance deal on the ground that the third party, and not Alliance, was the actual owner of the rights. When negotiations failed, TXO sued for a declaratory judgment that it had purchased the rights from the third party. The court found that TXO knew the action was frivolous, that it had unsuccessfully attempted to manufacture evidence in support of its claim, and that it had engaged in similar frauds in other states. Alliance counterclaimed for slander of title.

The jury awarded $19,000 in actual damages, the attorneys' fees for successfully defending the declaratory judgment action. And it awarded $10 million in punitive damages. The plurality upheld the award on the ground that the punitives were not disproportionate to the damage TXO might have caused, the loss of all future royalties. Justice Kennedy concurred on the ground that TXO acted with malice at the level of its senior officers. Justices Scalia and Thomas concurred on the grounds they offered in *BMW*. Justices O'Connor, White, and Souter dissented, principally on the ground that the plaintiff's final argument to a West Virginia jury openly appealed to bias against rich companies from Texas, and that there was no other record basis for the judgment. Neither side had noted the amount of the potential royalties in the state courts.

Page 692. After note 6, add:

The Supreme Court of Georgia has endorsed the provision in an opinion rejecting constitutional challenges to related legislation. Mack Trucks v. Conkle, 436 S.E.2d 635, 637-640 (Ga. 1993), further described supra at supplement to 676.

3. Punitive Damages in Contract

Page 702. After note 7, add:

7.1. The supreme court of Texas has attempted a major clarification of the standard for punitive damages generally and for bad faith breach in particular. Transportation Insurance Co. v. Moriel, 879 S.W.2d 10 (Tex. 1994). *Moriel* distinguishes three thresholds of liability: breach, yielding contract damages; bad faith breach, yielding tort damages, including emotional distress; and gross negligence, yielding punitive damages. In contrast to the usual hierarchies of language for describing fault, gross negligence here is worse than bad faith:

> [A]n insured claiming bad faith must prove that the insurer had no reasonable basis for denying or delaying payment of the claim, and that it knew or should have known that fact.
>
> [G]ross negligence includes two elements: (1) viewed from the standpoint of the actor, the act or omission must involve an extreme degree of risk, considering the probability and magnitude of the potential harm to others, and (2) the actor must have actual, subjective awareness of the risk involved, but nevertheless proceed in conscious indifference to the rights, safety, or welfare of others.

Id. at 18, 23. This definition of gross negligence apparently applies in all punitive damage cases. To recover punitives in a bad faith breach case, plaintiff must prove bad faith plus gross negligence. Delay, inconvenience, and emotional distress do not count as part of the serious potential harm component of the gross negligence standard; "death, grievous physical injury, or financial ruin" do count; apparently, forgone medical care counts. Id. at 23-24.

Is this a workable doctrinal structure? Try applying it to the bad faith claim in *TRANSCO*.

Page 703. After note 8, add:

9. Arbitrators may award punitive damages if implicitly or explicitly authorized by the contract that provides for arbitration. Mastrobuono v. Shearson Lehman Hutton, 115 S. Ct. 1212 (1995). In *Mastrobuono*, the contract provided for New York law, which provides that arbitrators cannot award punitives. But the contract also provided for arbitration under the rules of the National Association of Securities Dealers, which do authorize arbitrators to award punitives. Interpretation of the arbitration clause was a federal issue under the Federal Arbitration Act, 9 U.S.C. §1 et seq. (1988). The Court upheld an award of punitives, treating the reference to New York law as meaning New York law other than arbitration law.

B. OTHER PUNITIVE REMEDIES

2. Civil Penalties Payable to the Government

Page 707. After note 6, add:

6.1. The Court has extended its double jeopardy analysis to punitive taxes. Department of Revenue v. Kurth Ranch, 114 S. Ct. 1937 (1994). The Court invalidated a $1,000-per-ounce tax on possession or storage of marijuana, to be assessed within 72 hours after the taxpayer was arrested on criminal drug charges, and payable after the marijuana had been seized by the state and destroyed. The majority held that the tax was a punishment, and that it therefore could not be imposed in a second proceeding after a criminal conviction.

Chief Justice Rehnquist dissented on the ground that *Halper* should be limited to civil penalties and should not apply to taxes. Justice O'Connor dissented on the ground that the tax reasonably approximated the cost of enforcing the drug laws. Justice Scalia dissented on the ground that the double jeopardy clause does not apply to multiple punishments.

Page 708. After note 8, add:

8.1. The Court has held that property used in a crime can be forfeited even if the owner is innocent, and apparently even if the owner is the victim of the crime, so long as the owner voluntarily let the criminal take possession. Bennis v. Michigan, 116 S. Ct. 994 (1996). Bennis was half owner of a car in which her husband was caught with a prostitute. The state forfeited the car as a public nuisance; the majority seemed to think this was remedial, because it reduced neighborhood blight. The dissenters thought that it was obviously punitive, and that any punishment of an innocent owner was an excessive fine under Austin v. United States, described in note 7.

Bennis and BMW v. Gore were both decided five to four, with eight justices voting consistently for or against a substantive due process limit on civil punishment. The swing vote was Justice O'Connor, who has led the charge for limits on punitive damages but voted to uphold the forfeiture in *Bennis*.

8.2. The Court dramatically returned to older doctrine in United States v. Ursery, 64 U.S.L.W. 4565 (U.S., June 24, 1996). The Court held that civil forfeitures are not punishment for purposes of the double jeopardy clause, because they are in rem proceedings against the property. Thus, the government can prosecute criminally and also forfeit defendant's property in a separate, civil proceeding. The Court distinguished *Halper* and *Kurth* on the ground that civil penalties and taxes are not in rem, but instead impose personal liability on the defendant. The Court distinguished *Austin* on the ground that the excessive fines clause applies to all punishment—both civil and criminal and without a preliminary inquiry into whether the forfeiture was remedial or punitive—because such preliminary classifications would add nothing to the ultimate issue whether the fine was excessive.

The Court said that its rule was only a presumption, and that "where the 'clearest proof' indicates that an in rem civil forfeiture is 'so punitive either in purpose or effect' as to be equivalent to a criminal proceeding, that forfeiture may be subject to the Double Jeopardy Clause." Id. n.3, quoting United States v. One Assortment of 89 Firearms, 465 U.S. 354, 365 (1984). But it is hard to imagine a case that might trigger this protection if *Ursery* did not; Ursery forfeited his residence after police discovered marijuana inside; the marijuana had apparently been grown for home consumption by Ursery and his family. Justice Stevens, the lone dissenter, asked if during Prohibition the government could have forfeited every house in which somebody had a drink. Justices Souter, Kennedy, and Breyer joined the majority in *Ursery* after dissenting in *Bennis*; if they really believe that forfeitures are not punishment, it is hard to see why it mattered to them that the property owner was innocent.

The government sometimes gets substantial evidentiary and procedural advantages by pursuing separate civil and criminal proceedings. These advantages go to the heart of the double jeopardy protection against successive prosecutions. The Court did not consider those issues in *Ursery*, but it will be hard for defendants to argue that forfeitures are sometimes prosecutions if they are not even punishments. For powerful criticism of *Ursery*, see Susan Klein, Civil In Rem Forfeiture and Double Jeopardy, 82 Iowa L. Rev.—(forthcoming Oct. 1996).

CHAPTER 8

Ancillary Remedies

A. ENFORCING THE JUDGMENT

1. Enforcing Coercive Orders: The Contempt Power

a. The Three Kinds of Contempt

Page 712. Replace *Mine Workers*, Notes on the Three Kinds of Contempt, and Notes on Coercive Contempt, with the following:

INTERNATIONAL UNION, UNITED MINE WORKERS v. BAGWELL

114 S. Ct. 2552 (1994)

JUSTICE BLACKMUN delivered the opinion of the Court. . . .

I . . .

[T]he union engaged in a protracted labor dispute with . . . the companies over alleged unfair labor practices. In April 1989, the companies filed suit in the Circuit Court of Russell County, Virginia, to enjoin the union from conducting unlawful strike-related activities. The trial court entered an injunction which . . . prohibited the union and its members from . . . obstructing ingress and egress to company facilities, throwing objects at and physically threatening company employees, placing tire-damaging "jackrocks" on roads used by company vehicles, and picketing with more than a specified number of people at designated sites. . . .

On May 16, 1989, the trial court held a contempt hearing and found that petitioners had committed 72 violations of the injunction. After fining the union $642,000 for its disobedience, the court announced that it would fine the union $100,000 for any future violent breach of the injunction and $20,000 for any future nonviolent infraction . . .

In seven subsequent contempt hearings held between June and December 1989, the court found the union in contempt for more than four hundred separate violations of the injunction, many of them violent. . . . [E]ach contempt hearing was conducted as a civil proceeding before the trial judge, in which the parties conducted discovery, introduced evidence, and called and cross-examined witnesses. The trial court required that contumacious acts be proved beyond a reasonable doubt, but did not afford the union a right to jury trial.

As a result of these contempt proceedings, the court levied over $64,000,000 in fines against the union, approximately $12,000,000 of which was ordered payable to the companies. . . . [T]he court ordered that the remaining roughly $52,000,000 in fines be paid to the Commonwealth of Virginia and Russell and Dickenson Counties . . .

While appeals from the contempt orders were pending, the union and the companies settled the underlying labor dispute, agreed to vacate the contempt fines, and jointly moved to dismiss the case. A special mediator representing the Secretary of Labor, and the governments of Russell and Dickenson Counties, supported the parties' motion to vacate the outstanding fines. The trial court granted the motion to dismiss, dissolved the injunction, and vacated the $12,000,000 in fines payable to the companies. After reiterating its belief that the remaining $52,000,000 owed to the counties and the Commonwealth were coercive, civil fines, the trial court refused to vacate these fines . . .

[T]he court appointed respondent John L. Bagwell to act as Special Commissioner to collect the unpaid contempt fines on behalf of the counties and the Commonwealth.

The Court of Appeals of Virginia reversed and ordered that the contempt fines be vacated pursuant to the settlement agreement. 402 S.E.2d 899 (Va. App. 1991). . . .

[T]he Supreme Court of Virginia reversed. . . . Because the trial court's prospective fine schedule was intended to coerce compliance with the injunction and the union could avoid the fines through obedience, the court reasoned, the fines were civil and coercive and properly imposed in civil proceedings. 423 S.E.2d 349 (Va. 1992). . . .

II

A

"Criminal contempt is a crime in the ordinary sense," Bloom v. Illinois, 391 U.S. 194, 201 (1968), and "criminal penalties may not be imposed on someone who has not been afforded the protections that the Constitution requires of such criminal proceedings." Hicks v. Feiock, 485 U.S. 624, 632 (1988). . . . In contrast, civil contempt sanctions, or those penalties designed to compel future compliance with a court order, are considered to be coercive and avoidable through obedience, and thus may be imposed in an ordinary civil proceeding upon notice and an opportunity to be heard. Neither a jury trial nor proof beyond a reasonable doubt is required.

Although the procedural contours of the two forms of contempt are well established, the distinguishing characteristics of civil versus criminal contempts are somewhat less clear. In the leading early case addressing this issue in the context of imprisonment, the Court emphasized that whether a contempt is civil or criminal turns on the "character and purpose" of the sanction involved. Gompers v. Bucks Stove & Range Co., 221 U.S. 418, 441 (1911). Thus, a contempt sanction is considered civil if it "is remedial, and for the benefit of the complainant. But if it is for criminal contempt the sentence is punitive, to vindicate the authority of the court." Id.

As *Gompers* recognized, however, the stated purposes of a contempt sanction alone cannot be determinative. . . . Most contempt sanctions . . . to some extent punish a prior offense as well as coerce an offender's future obedience. The *Hicks* Court accordingly held that conclusions about the civil or criminal nature of a contempt sanction are properly drawn, not from "the subjective intent of a State's laws and its courts," 485 U.S. at 635, but "from an examination of the character of the relief itself," id. at 636.

The paradigmatic coercive, civil contempt sanction . . . involves confining a contemnor indefinitely until he complies with an affirmative command such as an order "to pay alimony, or to surrender property ordered to be turned over to a receiver, or to make a conveyance." 221 U.S. at 442. Imprisonment for a fixed term similarly is coercive when the contemnor is given the option of earlier release if he complies. In these circumstances, the contemnor is able to purge the contempt and obtain his release by committing an affirmative act, and thus "carries the keys of his prison in his own pocket." Id. at 442, quoting In re Nevitt, 117 F. 448, 461 (8th Cir. 1902).

By contrast, a fixed sentence of imprisonment is punitive and criminal if it is imposed retrospectively for a "completed act of disobedience," 221 U.S. at 443, such that the contemnor cannot avoid or abbreviate the confinement through later compliance. . . . "[T]he defendant is furnished no key, and he cannot shorten the term by promising not to repeat the offense." Id. at 442.

This dichotomy between coercive and punitive imprisonment has been extended to the fine context. A contempt fine accordingly is considered civil and remedial if it either "coerce[s] the defendant into compliance with the court's order, [or] . . . compensate[s] the complainant for losses sustained." United States v. United Mine Workers, 330 U.S. 258, 303-304 (1947). Where a fine is not compensatory, it is civil only if the contemnor is afforded an opportunity to purge. Thus, a "flat, unconditional fine" totalling even as little as $50 . . . is criminal if the contemnor has no subsequent opportunity to reduce or avoid the fine through compliance.

A close analogy to coercive imprisonment is a per diem fine imposed for each day a contemnor fails to comply with an affirmative court order. Like civil imprisonment, such fines exert a constant coercive pressure, and once the jural command is obeyed, the future, indefinite, daily fines are purged. Less comfortable is the analogy between coercive imprisonment and suspended, determinate fines. *Mine Workers* involved a $3,500,000 fine imposed against the union for nationwide . . . strike activities. Finding that the determinate fine was both criminal and excessive, the Court reduced the sanction to a flat criminal fine of $700,000. The Court then imposed and suspended the remaining $2,800,000 as a coercive civil fine, conditioned on the union's ability to purge the fine through full, timely compliance with the trial court's order.[4] The Court concluded, in light of this purge clause, that the civil fine operated as "a coercive imposition upon the defendant union to compel obedience with the court's outstanding order." 330 U.S. at 307.

This Court has not revisited the issue of coercive civil contempt fines addressed in *Mine Workers*. Since that decision, the Court has erected substantial procedural protections in other areas of contempt law, such as criminal contempts and summary contempts. Lower . . . courts . . . nevertheless have relied on *Mine Workers* to authorize a relatively unlimited judicial power to impose noncompensatory civil contempt fines.

B . . .

The traditional justification for the relative breadth of the contempt power has been necessity: Courts independently must be vested with "power to impose silence, respect, and decorum, in their presence, and submission to their lawful mandates, and . . . to preserve themselves and their officers from the approach and insults of pollution." Anderson v. Dunn, 19 U.S. (6 Wheat.) 204, 227 (1821). Courts thus have embraced an inherent contempt authority, as a power "necessary to the exercise of all others." United States v. Hudson, 11 U.S. (7 Cranch) 32, 34 (1812).

But the contempt power also uniquely is "liable to abuse." *Bloom*, 391 U.S. at 202, quoting Ex parte Terry, 128 U.S. 289, 313 (1888). Unlike most areas of law, where a legislature defines both the sanctionable conduct and the penalty to be imposed, civil contempt proceedings leave the offended judge solely responsible for identifying, prosecuting, adjudicating, and sanctioning the contumacious conduct. Contumacy "often strikes at the most vulnerable and human qualities of a judge's temperament," *Bloom*, 391 U.S. at 202, and its fusion of legislative, executive, and judicial powers "summons forth . . . the prospect of 'the most tyrannical licentiousness.'" Young v. United States ex rel. Vuitton et Fils, S.A., 481 U.S. 787, 822 (1987) (Scalia, J., concurring in judgment), quoting *Anderson*, 19 U.S. at 228. . . .

4. Although the size of the fine was substantial, the conduct required of the union to purge the suspended fine was relatively discrete. [The union was required to issue certain notices concerning the validity of a disputed labor contract.]

Our jurisprudence in the contempt area has attempted to balance the competing concerns of necessity and potential arbitrariness by allowing a relatively unencumbered contempt power when its exercise is most essential, and requiring progressively greater procedural protections when other considerations come into play. The necessity justification for the contempt authority is at its pinnacle, of course, where contumacious conduct threatens a court's immediate ability to conduct its proceedings, such as where a witness refuses to testify, or a party disrupts the court. . . . In light of the court's substantial interest in rapidly coercing compliance and restoring order, and because the contempt's occurrence before the court reduces the need for extensive factfinding and the likelihood of an erroneous deprivation, summary proceedings have been tolerated. . . .

If a court delays punishing a direct contempt [one committed in the presence of the court] until the completion of trial . . . due process requires that the contemnor's rights to notice and a hearing be respected. There "it is much more difficult to argue that action without notice or hearing of any kind is necessary to preserve order and enable [the court] to proceed with its business," Taylor v. Hayes, 418 U.S. 488, 498 (1974). . . . Direct contempts also cannot be punished with serious criminal penalties absent the full protections of a criminal jury trial. *Bloom*, 391 U.S. at 210.

Still further procedural protections are afforded for contempts occurring out of court . . . Summary adjudication of indirect contempts is prohibited, and criminal contempt sanctions are entitled to full criminal process. Certain indirect contempts nevertheless are appropriate for imposition through civil proceedings. Contempts such as failure to comply with document discovery, for example, while occurring outside the court's presence, impede the court's ability to adjudicate the proceedings before it and thus touch upon the core justification for the contempt power. Courts traditionally have broad authority through means other than contempt—such as by striking pleadings, assessing costs, excluding evidence, and entering default judgment—to penalize a party's failure to comply with the rules of conduct governing the litigation process. Such judicial sanctions never have been considered criminal, and the imposition of civil, coercive fines to police the litigation process appears consistent with this authority. Similarly, indirect contempts involving discrete, readily ascertainable acts, such as turning over a key or payment of a judgment, properly may be adjudicated through civil proceedings since the need for extensive, impartial factfinding is less pressing.

For a discrete category of indirect contempts, however, civil procedural protections may be insufficient. Contempts involving out-of-court disobedience to complex injunctions often require elaborate and reliable factfinding. Such contempts do not obstruct the court's ability to adjudicate the proceedings before it, and the risk of erroneous deprivation from the lack of a neutral factfinder may be substantial. Under these circumstances, criminal procedural protections such as the rights to counsel and proof beyond a reasonable doubt are both necessary and appropriate to protect the due process rights of parties and prevent the arbitrary exercise of judicial power.

C

In the instant case, neither any party nor any court of the Commonwealth has suggested that the challenged fines are compensatory. At no point did the trial court attempt to calibrate the fines to damages caused by the union's contumacious activities . . . The issue . . . is . . . whether these fines . . . are coercive civil or criminal sanctions. . . .

Petitioners argue that because the injunction primarily prohibited certain conduct rather than mandated affirmative acts, the sanctions are criminal. Respondent . . . urges that because the trial court established a prospective fine schedule that the union could avoid through compliance, the fines are civil . . .

Neither theory satisfactorily identifies those contempt fines that are criminal and thus must be imposed through the criminal process. . . .

[T]he distinction between coercion of affirmative acts and punishment of prohibited conduct is difficult to apply when conduct that can recur is involved, or when an injunction contains both mandatory and prohibitory provisions. Moreover, in borderline cases injunctive provisions containing essentially the same command can be phrased either in mandatory or prohibitory terms. Under a literal application of petitioners' theory, an injunction ordering the union: "Do not strike," would appear to be prohibitory and criminal, while an injunction ordering the union: "Continue working," would be mandatory and civil. In enforcing the present injunction, the trial court imposed fines without regard to the mandatory or prohibitory nature of the clause violated. . . . In a case like this involving an injunction that prescribes a detailed code of conduct, it is more appropriate to identify the character of the entire decree. Cf. *Hicks*, 485 U.S. at 639 n.10 (internal quotations omitted) (Where both civil and criminal relief is imposed "the criminal feature of the order is dominant and fixes its character for purposes of review"). . . .

Had the trial court simply levied the fines after finding the union guilty of contempt, the resulting "determinate and unconditional" fines would be considered "solely and exclusively punitive." *Hicks*, 485 U.S. at 632-633. Respondent nevertheless contends that the trial court's announcement of a prospective fine schedule allowed the union to "avoid paying the fine[s] simply by performing the . . . act required by the court's order," *Hicks*, 485 U.S. at 632, and thus transformed these fines into coercive, civil ones. . . .

[T]he fact that the trial court announced the fines before the contumacy, rather than after the fact, does not in itself justify respondent's conclusion that the fines are civil or meaningfully distinguish these penalties from the ordinary criminal law. Due process traditionally requires that criminal laws provide prior notice both of the conduct to be prohibited and of the sanction to be imposed. The trial court here simply announced the penalty—determinate fines of $20,000 or $100,000 per violation—that would be imposed for future contempts. The union's ability to avoid the contempt fines was indistinguishable from the ability of any ordinary citizen to avoid a criminal sanction by conforming his behavior to the law. The fines are not coercive day fines, or even suspended fines, but are more closely analogous to fixed, determinate, retrospective criminal fines which petitioners had no opportunity to purge once imposed. We therefore decline to conclude that the mere fact that the sanctions were announced in advance rendered them coercive and civil as a matter of constitutional law.

Other considerations convince us that the fines challenged here are criminal. The union's sanctionable conduct did not occur in the court's presence or otherwise implicate the court's ability to maintain order and adjudicate the proceedings before it. Nor did the union's contumacy involve simple, affirmative acts, such as the paradigmatic civil contempts examined in *Gompers*. Instead, the Virginia trial court levied contempt fines for widespread, ongoing, out-of-court violations of a complex injunction. In so doing, the court effectively policed petitioners' compliance with an entire code of conduct that the court itself had imposed. The union's contumacy lasted many months and spanned a substantial portion of the State. The fines assessed were serious, totalling over $52,000,000. Under such circumstances, disinterested factfinding and even-handed adjudication were essential, and petitioners were entitled to a criminal jury trial. . . .

III

The judgment of the Supreme Court of Virginia is reversed. . . .

JUSTICE SCALIA, concurring. . . .

That one and the same person should be able to make the rule, to adjudicate its violation, and to assess its penalty is out of accord with our usual notions of fairness and separation of powers. And it is worse still for that person to conduct the adjudication without affording the protections usually given in criminal trials. . . .

Incarceration until compliance was a distinctive sanction, and sheds light upon the nature of the decrees enforced by civil contempt. That sanction makes sense only if the order requires performance of an identifiable act (or perhaps cessation of continuing performance of an identifiable act). A general prohibition for the future does not lend itself to enforcement through conditional incarceration, since no single act (or the cessation of no single act) can demonstrate compliance and justify release. . . .

[In traditional equity practice,] [t]he mandatory injunctions issued upon termination of litigation usually required "a single simple act." Henry McClintock, Principles of Equity §15 at 32-33 (West 2d ed. 1948). Indeed, there was a "historical prejudice of the court of chancery against rendering decrees which called for more than a single affirmative act." Id. §61 at 160. And where specific performance of contracts was sought, it was the categorical rule that no decree would issue that required ongoing supervision. . . .

Even equitable decrees that were prohibitory rather than mandatory were, in earlier times, much less sweeping than their modern counterparts. Prior to the labor injunctions of the late 1800's, injunctions were issued primarily in relatively narrow disputes over property.

Contemporary courts have abandoned these earlier limitations upon the scope of their mandatory and injunctive decrees. They routinely issue complex decrees which involve them in extended disputes and place them in continuing supervisory roles over parties and institutions. See, e.g.,

Missouri v. Jenkins, 495 U.S. 33, 56-58 (1990); Swann v. Charlotte-Mecklenburg Board of Education, 402 U.S. 1, 16 (1971). . . .

When an order governs many aspects of a litigant's activities, rather than just a discrete act, determining compliance becomes much more difficult. Credibility issues arise, for which the factfinding protections of the criminal law (including jury trial) become much more important. And when continuing prohibitions or obligations are imposed, the order cannot be complied with (and the contempt "purged") in a single act; it continues to govern the party's behavior, on pain of punishment—not unlike the criminal law. . . .

The use of a civil process for contempt sanctions "makes no sense except as a consequence of historical practice." Weiss v. United States, 114 S. Ct. 752, 771 (1994) (Scalia, J., concurring in part). As the scope of injunctions has expanded, they have lost some of the distinctive features that made enforcement through civil process acceptable. It is not that the times, or our perceptions of fairness, have changed (that is in my view no basis for either tightening or relaxing the traditional demands of due process); but rather that the modern judicial order is in its relevant essentials not the same device that in former times could always be enforced by civil contempt. So adjustments will have to be made. We will have to decide at some point which modern injunctions sufficiently resemble their historical namesakes to warrant the same extraordinary means of enforcement. We need not draw that line in the present case, and so I am content to join the opinion of the Court.

JUSTICE GINSBURG, with whom CHIEF JUSTICE REHNQUIST joins, concurring . . .

II . . .

Two considerations persuade me that the contempt proceedings in this case should be classified as "criminal" rather than "civil." First, were we to accept the logic of Bagwell's argument that the fines here were civil, because "conditional" and "coercive," no fine would elude that categorization. The fines in this case were "conditional," Bagwell says, because they would not have been imposed if the unions had complied with the injunction. The fines would have been "conditional" in this sense, however, even if the court had not supplemented the injunction with its fines schedule; indeed, any fine is "conditional" upon compliance or noncompliance before its imposition. Furthermore, while the fines were "coercive," in the sense that one of their purposes was to encourage union compliance with the injunction, criminal contempt sanctions may also "coerce" in this same sense, for they, too, "ten[d] to prevent a repetition of the disobedience." *Gompers*, 221 U.S. at 443. . .

Second, the Virginia courts' refusal to vacate the fines, despite the parties' settlement and joint motion, is characteristic of criminal, not civil proceedings. . . . [W]ith the private complainant gone from the scene, and an official appointed by the Commonwealth to collect the fines for the Commonwealth's coffers, it is implausible to invoke the justification of benefiting the civil complainant. The Commonwealth here pursues the fines on its own account, not as the agent of a private party, and without tying the exactions exclusively to a claim for compensation. If, as the trial court declared, the proceedings were indeed civil from the outset, then the court should have granted the parties' motions to vacate the fines.

. . . I join the Court's judgment and all but Part II-B of its opinion.

NOTES ON THE THREE KINDS OF CONTEMPT

1. *Bagwell's* explanation of the traditional differences among criminal contempt, coercive civil contempt, and compensatory civil contempt was settled law in the federal courts and in most states. Even so, the reports are full of cases in which trial judges confused criminal contempt with coercive civil contempt. The most common error is to impose fixed penalties in civil proceedings, as in the first contempt hearing in *Bagwell.* The fines payable to the companies in *Bagwell* also suggest confusion: if they were coercive, they should have been payable to the government; if they were compensatory, the court should have required evidence of damages. In re Chase & Sanborn Corp., 872 F.2d 397 (11th Cir. 1989). The Supreme Court has emphasized that the distinctions depend entirely on the form of the sanctions, and not on the judge's purposes or motivations. Hicks v. Feiock, 485 U.S. 624, 631-637 (1985).

There is also a tendency to think that the distinction has to do with the nature of defendant's act—that some contempts are criminal and others civil. But the distinction is in the proceeding, not in the contempt. Any contempt can be the subject of civil or criminal proceedings or both, just like any assault and battery. The only difference that relates to defendant's act is the required state of mind: even inadvertent violations of the injunction are civil contempt, but only willful violations are criminal contempt. National Labor Relations Board v. Blevins Popcorn Co., 659 F.2d 1173, 1183-1184 (D.C. Cir. 1981).

2. *Criminal contempt.* Criminal contempt is criminal punishment for a past offense; the punishment is not conditional on future compliance. The prosecution may be begun by notice rather than indictment, but at trial, defendant gets substantially all the protections of criminal procedure, including proof beyond a reasonable doubt. The double jeopardy clause protects against separate prosecutions for criminal contempt and for an underlying criminal offense subsumed in the injunction, such as assault or jackrocking in *Bagwell.* United States v. Dixon, 509 U.S. 688 (1993). Defendant cannot constitutionally be sentenced to more than six months in jail without a jury trial, Bloom v. Illinois, 391 U.S. 194 (1968), and the federal courts of appeals have held that individuals cannot be fined more than $500 (perhaps somewhat more in the Eighth Circuit) without a jury trial. See Girard v. Goins, 575 F.2d 160, 165 (8th Cir. 1978). A state court recently rejected the $500 threshold as too small. State v. Simeona, 864 P.2d 1109 (Hawaii Ct. App. 1993).

Jury trial rights of corporations and labor unions apparently depend on case-by-case determinations of the seriousness of the fine in light of defendant's financial resources. See Muniz v. Hoffman, 422 U.S. 454 (1975), upholding a judge-imposed contempt fine of $10,000 against a local union, and United States v. Troxler Hosier Co., 681 F.2d 934 (4th Cir. 1982), upholding a judge-imposed contempt fine of $80,000. In Virginia, jury trial is required for any criminal contempt fine over $50. Va. Code Ann. §18.2-457 (1988).

The offense is complete when defendant willfully violates an injunction, even if the injunction is later held erroneous. Thus, defendant cannot challenge the validity of the injunction in a prosecution for criminal contempt. Walker v. City of Birmingham, 388 U.S. 307 (1967), infra at 747. This controversial rule is called the collateral bar rule, because it bars certain collateral attacks on the validity of injunctions.

Criminal contempt is prosecuted in the name of the sovereign; the civil plaintiff is in the position of a complaining witness. He can report the contempt, but he cannot require the court or prosecutor to proceed criminally, or stop them from continuing if he settles the case. Any fines are payable to the government.

3. *Civil contempt.* Civil contempt is prosecuted in the name of the plaintiff, and largely controlled by the plaintiff. He initiates it with a

motion, and up to a point he can abandon it or settle it; *Bagwell* turns in part on whether he eventually loses control. Violations must be proved by clear and convincing evidence. *Blevins Popcorn*, 659 F.2d at 1183-1184. The collateral bar rule does not apply, because the civil plaintiff is not entitled to benefit from an erroneous injunction.

a. *Compensatory civil contempt.* Compensatory civil contempt is like an action for damages or restitution. Despite the compensatory label, plaintiff can recover defendant's profits, at least if profits would be an appropriate measure of recovery for the underlying wrong. The leading case is Leman v. Krentler-Arnold Hinge Last Co., 284 U.S. 448 (1932), involving contempt of an injunction against patent infringement.

Because compensatory contempt is ancillary to the injunction suit, there is no jury trial in most jurisdictions. Partly for that reason, about ten states reject compensatory contempt, including California, Illinois, and Texas. Doug Rendleman, Compensatory Contempt: Plaintiff's Remedy When a Defendant Violates an Injunction, 1980 U. Ill. L.F. 971, 982-983 n.49. In those states, plaintiff must file an ordinary action for damages, an option that is also open in states that do have compensatory contempt. Plaintiff may want a jury too, or he may want to avoid the requirement of clear and convincing evidence that is generally applied in contempt. Does that evidentiary standard make any sense in compensatory contempt?

There is a doctrinal irony in compensatory contempt. Before it issued the injunction, the court decided that damages would be an inadequate remedy. Damages are inadequate, but they are not useless; recall that adequacy is relative. In any event, damages are now the best the court can do.

b. *Coercive contempt.* Criminal contempt looks much like ordinary punishment, and compensatory contempt looks much like ordinary compensation. The unique contribution of the contempt power is coercive civil contempt. Before exploring coercive contempt, there is one more question applicable to both coercive and criminal contempt.

4. In *Bagwell*, a special commissioner was appointed to collect the fines. This is necessary in civil contempt only when the civil plaintiff attempts to settle the case, and perhaps it is always illegitimate, as Justice Ginsburg implies. It is more common in criminal contempt. The court may ask the prosecutor to prosecute the contempt, or it may appoint any member of the bar as special prosecutor. Federal courts may appoint a special prosecutor only if the United States Attorney declines to

prosecute. Young v. United States ex rel. Vuitton et Fils S.A., 481 U.S. 787 (1987). *Young* and many states reject the practice of appointing plaintiff's attorney as special prosecutor; she owes duties to her client that will sometimes conflict with the proper exercise of prosecutorial discretion.

NOTES ON COERCIVE CONTEMPT

1. Coercive contempt depends on a conditional penalty; defendant is coerced to comply because the penalty will be bigger if he doesn't. In *Bagwell*, the court specified conditional fines before the violations, and tried to collect them after the violations. Does collection of such fines now require criminal procedure in all cases? Only where the facts are complex? Only where the fines are large? Can you state the constitutional rule announced in *Bagwell*?

2. When conditional fines are used for coercive contempt, the process breaks into three distinct steps. The third step is not easily pigeonholed. When the court threatened to fine the union $100,000 for each violent violation, the threat was remedial and prospective. After the threats had failed, enforcing the fines looks punitive and retrospective. The fines had lost their coercive effect; they were no longer conditional, because the condition had been fulfilled. But the law must keep its promises, or coercive contempt will no longer coerce. Coercive fines must be collected, but they need not be collected with civil procedure.

3. Everyone agrees that the unconditional fines at the first contempt hearing, imposed as punishment for past violations, were criminal. The fines for later violations were allegedly different because the judge threatened them at the first hearing, and the union could have avoided them by obeying the injunction.

On that scenario, what was the purpose of the second step of coercive contempt? When the court issues an injunction, defendant knows he can be fined or imprisoned for violating it. When the court finds defendant in contempt and announces a coercive sanction, it specifies the future penalty. What does that add to the injunction? If telling defendant what the penalty is going to be makes injunctions more effective, why not tell him when the injunction is issued? Is there any need to wait for a violation before specifying the penalty?

4. The three steps of coercive contempt are even more puzzling if the court is not bound to impose the penalty it threatened. In *Bagwell*, the judge had threatened to double the fines every day. He appears to have imposed more than $100,000 per violation, but only a tiny fraction of that amount doubled daily. Why threaten a particular penalty, if the threat itself can be unlimited for all practical purposes, and if the actual penalty has no necessary relation to the threatened penalty? One court has said that a judge at the third step of coercive contempt "should not feel bound in any way by the specific amount" threatened at the second step. Labor Relations Commission v. Fall River Education Association, 416 N.E.2d 1340, 1350 (Mass. 1981). Can that be right? Does the second step serve any purpose in that scenario?

5. Defendant's wealth is relevant to the size of coercive fines; the court must ask how much it takes to deter *this* defendant. Fines per day or per violation increase the difficulty of assessing ability to pay. When the trial court in *Bagwell* said $100,000 per violent violation, it did not anticipate 400 violations. If it set the fine at $10,000, so the union could reasonably afford 400 violations, would it be inviting 400 violations? Isn't plaintiff entitled to a fine that will deter immediately? Does it defeat the purpose if defendant is entitled to have that fine reduced if it accumulates to unduly burdensome levels? Of course, if the fine accumulates beyond the amount of defendant's net worth plus foreseeable income, further accumulations are meaningless anyway.

6. The original and simplest form of coercive contempt is to imprison the contemnor until he complies. This avoids the conundrums of three-step coercive contempt. There are only two steps: First the injunction is issued, and then defendant is found in contempt and sent to jail. Conditional penalties do not accumulate to be collected later, because imprisonment is continuous. Every instant he refuses to comply, and every instant he remains in prison for that refusal.

But imprisonment has disadvantages. Some injunctions can be obeyed only if defendant is at large. In *Blevins Popcorn*, the court was trying to force an employer to bargain with its employees' union. It can't very well bargain if its officers are in prison. At best the court can imprison them until they promise to bargain, and then let them out and see if the fear of returning to prison induces them to keep their promise. Imprisonment is expensive to the state, especially if there are many contemnors. Imprisoning a few leaders may create martyrs; few judges have been willing to imprison the rank and file.

7. There is psychology and gamesmanship in coercive contempt; moderate threats may be more effective than harsher threats. A threat should not be so great that the contemnor doubts the court's will to carry it out, or so great that there is no room for further escalation. In strike cases, and other cases where the litigants have a continuing relationship, harsh sanctions may end the contempt but ruin the relationship.

Such tactical considerations may explain the three steps of coercive fines. Indeed, some judges have stretched the contempt process out into an indefinite number of steps, especially in structural injunctions against government defendants. Early contempt proceedings may result not in a finding of contempt, but in a clarification of the order, making it more specific. Or the court may find defendants in contempt, and indicate that they may purge themselves of contempt by doing A, B, and C, which turn out to be more detailed specifications of the obligations of the original injunction. The court can continue this process indefinitely, slowly tightening the screws.

8. The principal alternative to the injunction in *Bagwell* would have been criminal prosecution for each act of violence. That would have required identifying the individual perpetrators, who were presumably unknown in many cases. It would have required full criminal trials; the court could not have adjudicated more than 400 violations in eight hearings lasting only one or two days each, which is how it adjudicated the contempt citations. And defendants would have been entitled to jury trial. The pool of potential jurors was presumably divided over the strike; the risk of hung juries might have been substantial.

Conceivably the union as an organization could have been criminally prosecuted for conspiracy, and then found guilty of substantive offenses pursuant to the conspiracy without identifying individual perpetrators. Such a prosecution would be at the frontiers of conspiracy law, it would have required full criminal jury trial, and except for attempted murder, the maximum fine would appear to be $2,500 per felony or serious misdemeanor. Va. Code Ann. §§18.2-10, 18.2-11 (Supp. 1995). The maximum fine for attempted murder would be $100,000. See §18.2-26 (1988). Jackrocking is a class 1 misdemeanor, §18.2-147.2 (1988), punishable by a fine of $2,500. Human perpetrators could of course be imprisoned, but fines are the only criminal penalty that could be applied to the union as an entity.

9. Were the contempt fines in *Bagwell* necessary because the criminal process was wholly inadequate to protect the rights of the companies and

their replacement workers, including their right to life and physical safety? Or were these fines a massive circumvention of hard-won procedural protections against excessive penalties and judicial abuse? Might they be both? "Government by injunction"—the use of injunctions to bypass juries, increase penalties, and sometimes create new substantive prohibitions, especially in the context of labor strife—was a major and recurring political issue from 1896 to 1932. Most of the story is told in Felix Frankfurter and Nathan Greene, The Labor Injunction (Macmillan 1930). In 1932, Congress enacted the Norris-LaGuardia Act, 29 U.S.C. §§101 et seq. (1994), which deprives federal courts of jurisdiction to enjoin strikes; the Act does not prevent federal injunctions against the unlawful tactics at issue in *Bagwell.*

10. If you think the fines in *Bagwell* are abusively large, is that an argument for retaining the irreparable injury rule? Is there any chance whatever that the trial judge would have found no irreparable injury in *Bagwell*? Don't we have to address any abuses directly, and not with an easily rebutted presumption against issuing injunctions in the first place?

A corollary of the irreparable injury rule is that equity will not enjoin a crime. This rule was designed to confine criminal matters to the criminal process, but it too has been swallowed by its exceptions. Criminal prosecution is an inadequate remedy if the penalties are too small to deter, or if the threatened crime is so serious that no violations can be tolerated. The rule does not apply if the criminal penalties are incidental to a primary enforcement procedure that is administrative, or if the crime is also a nuisance or a tort. What does that leave? The cases are collected in Douglas Laycock, The Death of the Irreparable Injury Rule 217-220 (Oxford 1991).

11. You may need to know a bit of labor law to understand the bitterness of the underlying dispute in *Bagwell.* The replacement workers were not just strikebreakers; they were potentially permanent replacements. If the union lost on its claim that the strike was in response to unfair labor practices, the company could retain its replacements permanently, and the strikers would be entitled to be rehired only as openings arose through attrition or expansion. National Labor Relations Board v. Mackay Radio & Telegraph Co., 304 U.S. 333, 345-347 (1938). The right to permanently replace strikers is not new, but until recently, employers were rarely able to take full advantage of it. Economic and technological changes, including the decline of union members as a percentage of the workforce, automated operations that reduce the number

of workers and skill levels required, and the increasing pressure of international competition, have made permanent replacement a viable option for many employers.

Unions have always viewed the right to permanent replacement as wholly illegitimate, a feature of U.S. labor law found in no other industrialized democracy. The Mine Workers have a long tradition of defying laws they consider illegitimate. So the strikers in *Bagwell* viewed themselves not just as trying to win a pay raise, but as protecting their jobs from permanent loss to usurpers.

Page 735. After the end of the second paragraph of note 6, add:

Yahiya Avraham died in prison at the age of 81; his widow was 66. They were married when she was 12, and separated when she was 22. Los Angeles Times at A4 (Dec. 6, 1994).

Page 744. After the first paragraph of note 5, add:

The Supreme Court unanimously applied this rule in Kokkonen v. Guardian Life Insurance Co., 114 S. Ct. 1673 (1994), holding that federal courts have no jurisdiction to enforce a settlement agreement that resulted in dismissal of a federal lawsuit. The Court noted that if the parties wanted federal enforcement in the original lawsuit, they could have embodied their agreement in a consent decree, or what the Court treated as the equivalent, provided that the court retained jurisdiction to enforce the contract. Failing that, the only remedy was a new suit in state court for breach of contract.

The Prison Litigation Reform Act takes advantage of this rule to provide that no consent decree can be entered in federal prison litigation without findings sufficient to support a litigated decree. But the Act notes that the parties can enter into "a private settlement agreement" enforceable in a state law contract action. For further analysis, see supra at supplement to 326.

2. Collecting Money Judgments

a. Execution, Garnishment, and the Like

Page 790. After the first paragraph of note 1, add:

Execution sales are generally conducted at auction on the courthouse steps, with advertising only in the legal notices section of the newspaper; they generally bring prices far below value. Mortgage foreclosures suffer from similar problems. The Supreme Court recently held that fair market value of the property is irrelevant to determining its value in a foreclosure sale; the price received at a procedurally correct and noncollusive foreclosure sale is irrebuttably the value of the property. BFP v. Resolution Trust Corp., 114 S. Ct. 1757 (1994). The issue arose when the debtor's trustee in bankruptcy attempted to recover for other creditors the property sold at the foreclosure sale. The trustee argued that the sale had been for less than reasonably equivalent value, and therefore was a fraudulent transfer. For more on fraudulent transfers, see the main volume at 626. (The notes at 626 use the older term, "fraudulent conveyance.")

Page 801. After note 6, add:

7. The legal means of collection are largely ineffective against debtors with few or no nonexempt assets. Many creditors traditionally tried threatening or harassing debtors until they paid. With respect to consumer debt, most of these techniques are barred by the Fair Debt Collection Practices Act, 15 U.S.C. §§1692 et seq. (1994). Any deception of the debtor is also a violation. The Supreme Court recently held that attorneys representing creditors are subject to the Act, Heintz v. Jenkins, 115 S. Ct. 1489 (1995), and thus liable for actual and statutory damages plus attorneys' fees.

8. Federal courts have jurisdiction to use all the available means of collection to collect federal judgments, including efforts to reach defendant's assets in the hands of third parties. But a claim that an additional defendant, not named in the judgment, is personally liable on the underlying claim, as in a suit to pierce the corporate veil of the original defendant, is a new lawsuit that requires an independent basis for federal jurisdiction. Peacock v. Thomas, 116 S. Ct. 862 (1996).

Page 802. At the end of the Note on Bankruptcy, add:

The Supreme Court faced an important practical issue at the intersection of bankruptcy, collections, and appellate procedure, but resolved only part of it. Celotex Corp. v. Edwards, 115 S. Ct. 1493 (1995).

Appellants who want to stay collection of a money judgment must file a bond, generally called a supersedeas bond, in the full amount of the judgment plus interest. Plaintiffs got a large judgment against Celotex, a manufacturer of asbestos. Celotex filed a supersedeas bond and an appeal. The insurer that issued the bond secured its right to reimbursement by holding money that it owed Celotex from another transaction. The judgment was affirmed, and Celotex filed for bankruptcy. Plaintiffs sued the insurer to collect on the bond, but the bankruptcy court enjoined the suit against the insurer.

The Court decided that plaintiffs must obey the injunction, citing Walker v. City of Birmingham (see 747 in the main volume). Plaintiffs could present their claim on the bond to the bankruptcy court, where Celotex was arguing that the bond was invalid. The Court expressed no view on whether the bond was enforceable in bankruptcy.

The principal risk that supersedeas bonds protect from is that the judgment will become uncollectible by the time the appeal is decided. If defendant's subsequent bankruptcy makes the bond unenforceable, what is the point of the bond? From Celotex's perspective, plaintiffs' judgment would be an unsecured claim in bankruptcy, presumably to be paid only in part; if plaintiffs collect in full on the bond, the insurer's secured claim will be substituted, and it will have to be paid in full. Celotex had over 100 appeals pending and $70 million in supersedeas bonds outstanding. But isn't the point of the bond requirement precisely to secure plaintiffs' claim?

Page 803. After note 3, add:

The Seventh Circuit en banc has now entirely vacated the *Evans* consent decree. 10 F.3d 474 (7th Cir. 1994). For more on this decision, see supplement to 326.

Page 804. After note 4, add:

For a careful exploration of the problems of collecting judgments from financially distressed municipalities, see Michael W. McConnell and Randal C. Picker, When Cities Go Broke: A Conceptual Introduction to Municipal Bankruptcy, 60 U. Chi. L. Rev. 425 (1993).

b. Coercive Collection of Money

Page 816. After the second paragraph of note 9, add:

The Supreme Court has agreed to decide whether custodial parents can sue inept state agencies who fail to make reasonable efforts to collect child support. Freestone v. Cowan, 68 F.3d 1141 (9th Cir. 1995), *cert. granted as* Blessing v. Freestone, 116 S. Ct. 1671 (1996). Defendant state officials argue that the federal statute creates no enforceable right, that monitoring by the federal executive is the exclusive remedy, and that such a suit violates core principles of federalism and separation of powers. The opinion of the court of appeals collects the conflicting decisions of the various circuits.

Page 818. After note 13, add:

13.1. An Oklahoma statute authorized judges to order defendants to pay judgments in installments out of nonexempt income, and to enforce the order with the contempt power. 12 Okla. Stat. §850 (1991). The state court struck down the contempt provision as violating the state prohibition on imprisonment for debt. Lepak v. McClain, 844 P.2d 852 (Okla. 1992). *Lepak* does not just create a defense of inability to pay; it apparently strikes down any use of the contempt power. *Lepak* effectively overrules a decision upholding the statute, Freeman v. Heiman, 426 F.2d 1050 (10th Cir. 1970). *Freeman* collects older cases upholding such statutes in other states.

B. LITIGATION EXPENSES

Page 846. After note 1, add:

1.1. How explicitly must Congress authorize attorneys' fees? That was the question in Key Tronic Corp. v. United States, 114 S. Ct. 1960 (1994). A statute creating liability for the costs of cleaning up polluted sites authorized recovery of "any other cost of response," and response was defined to include "enforcement activities related thereto." Comprehensive Environmental Response, Compensation, and Liability Act of 1980 (CERCLA), 42 U.S.C. §§9607(a)(4)(B), 9601(25) (1988). The majority thought that "enforcement activities" was insufficiently explicit to override the American rule with respect to fees for litigation and negotiation aimed at reallocating the costs of the cleanup. Justice Scalia for three dissenters thought that attorneys' fees were the obvious and principle cost of "enforcement activities."

The Court unanimously held that the statute did authorize attorneys' fees for investigations aimed at discovering other responsible parties, because these fees increased the likelihood of a successful cleanup. The Court also said that because they were not incurred in litigation, they were not subject to the American rule.

Page 847. After the first paragraph of note 3, add:

The summary of Chambers v. NASCO is not quite right. The Court did emphasize that defendant had been punished for litigation conduct and not for substantive conduct, and that the sanctions were therefore consistent both with *Alyeska* and with Erie R.R. v. Tompkins, 304 U.S. 64 (1938). But the Court kept its options open with the following footnote: "We therefore express no opinion as to whether the District Court would have had the inherent power to sanction Chambers for conduct relating to the underlying breach of contract, or whether such sanctions might implicate the concerns of *Erie*." 501 U.S. 32, 54 n.16 (1991).

Page 852. After note 6, add:

7. The Copyright Act authorizes "a reasonable attorney's fee to the prevailing party," 17 U.S.C. §505 (1994), language indistinguishable from

the civil rights provision construed in *Christiansburg*. But the Court has rejected one-way fee shifting under the Copyright Act. Fogarty v. Fantasy, Inc., 114 S. Ct. 1023 (1994). (Fogarty, the successful defendant, was the lead singer for Creedence Clearwater Revival, a sixties group that middle-aged faculty will remember.)

The Court said that civil rights cases often involve impecunious plaintiffs suing defendants with far more resources, but that in copyright cases, both plaintiffs and defendants "run the gamut from corporate behemoths to starving artists." Id. at 1028, quoting Cohen v. Virginia Electric & Power Co., 617 F. Supp. 619, 622-623 (E.D. Va. 1985). The Court also said that the amount in controversy in copyright cases is often small, and that this is especially true on the defendant's side, 114 S. Ct. at 1030, quoting Arthur Weil, American Copyright Law (Callaghan 1917), but it did not appear to rely on this assertion.

The Court also rejected presumptive two-way fee shifting. Rather, it said that trial courts should exercise their discretion "in light of the considerations we have identified," 114 S. Ct. at 1033, quoting Hensley v. Eckerhart, 461 U.S. 424, 437 (1983), and that this discretion should be exercised evenhandedly between plaintiffs and defendants. Should district courts now expressly take account of the relative resources of plaintiff and defendant?

8. For a straightforward analysis of the theoretical case for and against one-way fee shifting, see Harold J. Krent, Explaining One-Way Fee Shifting, 79 Va. L. Rev. 2039 (1993). Professor Krent unsurprisingly concludes that one-way fee shifting is most valuable where it enables plaintiffs of modest means to pursue claims with modest stakes.

Page 854. After note 3, add:

The Fourth Circuit has read Farrar v. Hobby, described in note 2 at 852, to repudiate the catalyst theory. S-1 v. State Board of Education, 21 F.3d 49 (4th Cir. 1994) (en banc). The First, Third, Fifth, Sixth, and Tenth Circuits disagree; the cases are collected in Baumgartner v. Harrisburg Housing Authority, 21 F.3d 541 (3d Cir. 1994).

Page 870. After note 1, add:

1.1. Some states give medical providers a lien on their patients' personal injury judgments. The New Mexico court has held that a hospital that collects out of such a lien is liable for its proportionate share of plaintiff's attorneys' fees. Moreover, the court apparently intends that the patient's liability to the hospital will be discharged. Martinez v. St. Joseph Healthcare System, 871 P.2d 1363 (N.M. 1994). The court distinguished a number of decisions in other states, all apparently holding that medical providers are not liable for any part of plaintiff's attorneys' fees. For another decision following *Martinez*, see In re Guardianship of Bloomquist, 523 N.W.2d 352 (Neb. 1994).

Page 872. After note 2, add:

2.1. In In re Washington Public Power Supply System Securities Litigation, 19 F.3d 1291 (9th Cir. 1994), the settlement was $687 million, allegedly the largest securities fraud settlement ever. The court calculated fees by the lodestar, because "the size of the fund magnified beyond all reasonable limits the margin of error inherent in a percentage fee award." Id. at 1297. And it directed the district court to allow a contingency enhancement, holding that *Dague* does not apply to common fund cases even when the lodestar is used. The opinion collects the cases on each of these issues. The rejection of *Dague* in common fund cases appears quite general. Most circuits leave the choice between lodestar and percentage of recovery to case-by-case discretion in common fund cases, but the Eleventh and D.C. Circuits require percentage fees.

Page 886. After note 6, add:

6.1. A California court has addressed the problem of simultaneous negotiation in an individual case where the attorney negotiated $150,000 for the client and $215,000 for himself. Ramirez v. Sturdevant, 26 Cal. Rptr. 2d 554 (Cal. Ct. App. 1994). The tenor of the opinion is radically different from *Evans*, which is not cited. The California court approved simultaneous negotiation of separate settlements for damages and fees, and it did not require the attorney to give the client a veto or to subordinate his interests to the client's. The court was "not unsympathetic to the need and desire of attorneys to settle actions in such a manner as to protect their own interests in addition to those of the client." Id. at 563. The court approved the attorney's insistence that the client sign a contract promising to accept any settlement of $150,000 or more, because that was a reasonable settlement figure and because attorneys have ample reason to be "concerned that the client might reject a reasonable settlement offer." Id. at 561.

However, the court recognized the inherent conflict of interest in simultaneous negotiation, and adopted a procedure by analogy from judicial approval of class action settlements. The trial court must approve the settlement, in a proceeding at which it would be presumed that the conflict of interest harmed the client. The court is not to decide whether the settlement reflects the full value of the case or is fair as between plaintiff and defendant, but only whether the settlement was "tainted by the conflict of interest," or in another formulation, whether the negotiations reflected "a fair and reasonable balancing of the interests" of the attorney and his client. Id. at 566. It seems unlikely that this procedure will work very well, but it might at least catch the most egregious abuses by attorneys. Is that the best we can do?

6.2. The supreme court of Texas has held that no class action settlement can be approved unless the class is notified of the maximum amount of fees that might be awarded to class counsel. General Motors Corp. v. Bloyed, 916 S.W.2d 949, 958-961 (Tex. 1996).

Page 887. After note 9, add:

9.1. Professor Coffee has extended his analysis in light of recent events in the courts. John C. Coffee, Jr., Class Wars: The Dilemma of the Mass Tort Class Action, 95 Colum. L. Rev. 1343 (1995). Some of the worst abuses in traditional class actions cumulating many modest claims are scrip settlements, in which the attorneys' fees are paid in cash but the class members get discount coupons for future purchases of defendant's products, and cy pres settlements, in which the class members get nothing but defendant pays attorneys' fees and contributes to a charity.

Abuses with larger stakes have emerged in mass tort litigation, where the sheer burden of many large claims has led courts to experiment with mass tort class actions. Class actions combining individual claims that are large rather than small has fundamentally changed the incentives on the actors in the system. In these cases, defendants seek class certification instead of opposing it, seek the largest possible definition of the class so as to bind as many plaintiffs as possible, and seek out the plaintiffs' attorney who will accept the cheapest settlement. Honest lawyers on the plaintiffs' side work at the enormous risk that the least scrupulous lawyer will settle the class out from under them. The traditional attack on the class action was that it blackmailed defendants; now the most telling criticism is that defendants have learned how to use it to deprive plaintiffs of their rights.

The worst abuses tend to come in settlement classes, in which the class is certified only for purposes of settlement, without a finding that the case could be tried as a class action. Present claimants with existing injuries, and unidentifiable future claimants who will eventually have injuries, are sometimes combined into a single class that settles for a fixed sum. The lawyers get paid, the present claimants get paid something, and the future claimants are bound whether or not there is enough left in the settlement fund for reasonable compensation when their claims finally arise. The evidence of implicit and explicit collusion between defendants and attorneys for the class seems clear in at least some of these cases. Courts have disapproved some of these settlements, but desperation to clear the docket has led courts to approve many of them. The article is convincing that existing safeguards are insufficient to protect class members, and indeed, that all the incentives are pushing the wrong way.

9.2. A state-court settlement is binding in federal court to the same extent it binds in the courts of the state that approved the settlement, even if the settlement released federal claims over which the state courts lacked jurisdiction. Matsushita Electric Industrial Co. v. Epstein, 116 S. Ct. 873 (1996). But any class action settlement is open to attack on the ground that the class representatives failed to adequately represent the class. Richards v. Jefferson County, 116 S. Ct. 1761 (1996). Most of the successful collateral attacks on class settlements have involved failure to observe basic formalities or obvious and egregious conflicts of interest; the doctrine is not yet tested against the more recent pattern of collusive settlements. Judges will predictably be reluctant to restore large numbers of settled claims to the docket; they may be even less willing to find inadequate representation on collateral attack than to disapprove inadequate settlements in the first place.

CHAPTER 9

Remedial Defenses

D. LACHES AND LIMITATIONS

2. Statutes of Limitations

Page 940. After note 2, add:

The judgment was affirmed by an equally divided Court. Morgan Stanley & Co. v. Pacific Mutual Life Insurance Co., 114 S. Ct. 1827 (1994). When the Court took the issue up again, it held that Congress has no power to direct the reopening of final judgments. Plaut v. Spendthrift Farms, 115 S. Ct. 1446 (1995). Nothing in the opinion implies that the statute is invalid as applied to cases that were pending when the statute was enacted.

The Court has also said that for federal statutes enacted before 1990, reference to the analogous state statute of limitations remains the norm, and that reference to an analogous federal statute of limitations is exceptional. North Star Steel Co. v. Thomas, 115 S. Ct. 1927 (1995). In *North Star*, the arguably analogous federal statute was only sixty days.

Page 950. After note 9, add:

10. The Supreme Court has agreed to decide whether the federal statute of limitations on suits for tax refunds, 26 U.S.C. §6511(b) (1994), is subject to equitable tolling. Brockamp v. United States, 67 F.3d 260 (9th Cir. 1995), *cert. granted*, 116 S. Ct. 1875 (1996). The asserted ground for tolling is not the discovery rule, but mental incompetence. A 93-year-old taxpayer sent a $7,000 check to the IRS with a request for the automatic extension of time to file his return. He died at age 98 without having filed the return. His daughter then discovered the check and filed the return, showing a tax liability of $427, and explaining that her father had been senile. The government refused a refund and pled limitations.

11. The Court has also agreed to decide what triggers the statute of limitations for civil RICO actions. Grimmett v. Brown, 75 F.3d 506 (9th Cir.), *cert. granted*, 64 U.S.L.W. 3830 (June 17, 1996). RICO, the Racketeer Influenced and Corrupt Organizations Act, imposes liability for injuries caused by a pattern of certain illegal acts known as "predicate offenses." Is it enough that plaintiff knows she was injured, or must she also know that there was a pattern? Must she know defendants' identity? Must she be able to quantify her damages? Plaintiff is an ex-wife who says her ex-husband and his bankruptcy lawyer swindled her out of her community property interest in his medical practice.

Page 958. After note 9, add:

9.1. For a spectacular fraudulent concealment case, see Allred v. Chynoweth, 990 F.2d 527 (10th Cir. 1993). Chynoweth was a member of a polygamous religious group. In 1977, she murdered Rulon Allred, the leader of a rival polygamous group. She acted at the direction of her group's leader, who was later convicted of murder. Chynoweth was also charged with murder, but she took the stand and denied the crime, and a jury acquitted her in 1979. In 1990, she published a book about her experiences, and in the book, she confessed to the murder. Plaintiffs promptly sued for wrongful death.

The majority held that Chynoweth had fraudulently concealed the cause of action by her perjury and by wearing a disguise at the crime scene, thus precluding eyewitness identification. Judge McKay, dissenting, argued that plaintiffs learned of their claim in the late 1970s. He thought the evidence that led to Chynoweth's prosecution gave them ample ground to sue, and that her acquittal on a reasonable-doubt standard was irrelevant to whether they should have proceeded with a civil suit to be decided by a preponderance of the evidence.

CHAPTER 10

Remedies and Separation of Powers

A. IMPLIED RIGHTS OF ACTION

Page 976. After note 2, add:

The Court refused to imply a right, under Securities and Exchange Commission Rule 10b-5, to sue aiders and abetters of securities fraud. Central Bank v. First Interstate Bank, 114 S. Ct. 1439 (1994). The right of action was long and well established in the lower courts, but the Supreme Court had never passed on the issue.

Page 978. After note 7, add:

When Congress does provide some explicit remedy, the Court usually treats that as reason not to imply any different or additional remedy. Thus, where the Resource Conservation and Recovery Act, 42 U.S.C. §6972 et seq. (1994), authorized injunctions ordering previous owners of land to clean up dangerous pollution on the site, the Court would not imply a right of the present owner to clean up the site and sue for reimbursement. Meghrig v. KFC Western, 116 S. Ct. 1251 (1996).

B. INITIATING CRIMINAL AND ADMINISTRATIVE REMEDIES

Page 992. After note 8, add:

8.1. Consider Livadas v. Bradshaw, 114 S. Ct. 2068 (1994). California law requires employers to pay discharged employees in full on the day of discharge. If payment is delayed, the employer must pay one day's wages for each day of delay, and the state labor commissioner is required to collect this penalty for the employee. The commissioner refused to collect the penalty for any employee covered by a collective bargaining agreement with an arbitration clause. Plaintiff in *Livadas* successfully sued the commissioner in federal court to force her to collect the penalty.

The Supreme Court unanimously held that the commissioner's policy discriminated against the federal right to bargain collectively, and that plaintiff could sue under 42 U.S.C. §1983 (1994), which creates a cause of action for violations of federal law by state officials. It appears that no one raised a standing issue, and the opinion does not mention *Linda R.S.*, *Simon*, *Allen*, or *Heckler*. Was this just an oversight? Or is the key to *Livadas* that the money collected by the commissioner would be paid over to plaintiff?

C. GOVERNMENTAL IMMUNITIES

1. Suits against the Government

Page 1005. After note 10, add:

11. Massachusetts has prospectively abolished the public duty doctrine. Jean W. v. Commonwealth, 610 N.E.2d 305 (Mass. 1993). The badly divided opinions review experience with the doctrine in Massachusetts and collect cases from around the country. Justice Wilkins, concurring, predicted that equally difficult line-drawing problems will promptly emerge with respect to causation. Id. at 316.

The legislature responded by codifying the principal applications of the public duty doctrine. Mass. Gen. Laws Ann. ch. 258, §10 (West Supp.

1996). There is no liability for issuing or failing to issue licenses, for negligent inspections, for release or escape of prisoners unless gross negligence is shown, for failures of police or fire protection unless the victim relied on "explicit and specific assurances of safety or assistance," or for failure to diminish the harmful consequences of conditions or situations not originally caused by the government or its employees.

This last category, failure to diminish harm caused by others, is subject to four exceptions in which immunity is waived: (1) reliance on explicit and specific assurances, (2) intervention that "causes injury to the victim or places the victim in a worse position than he was in before the intervention," (3) any claim based on negligent maintenance of public property, and (4) medical malpractice by government employees. Is that a workable set of rules? Do the distinctions make policy sense?

12. Compare Allison Gas Turbine Division v. District of Columbia, 642 A.2d 841 (D.C. 1994). Police ordered civilian scuba divers out of the water at the scene of a helicopter crash in the Potomac River, even though the divers had already rescued one victim, and even though the police divers did not have their equipment with them. When the equipment arrived twenty minutes later, the remaining three victims were dead. The D.C. court held that the duty to conduct rescues runs to the general public and not to individual victims, that the order to the civilian divers was part of the performance of that general duty, and that therefore the order precluding civilian rescue created no duty to the victims. The court also commented that the officers had no way to know whether the civilian divers were qualified, and that they might have feared liability if the civilian divers were themselves killed or injured. Would that case proceed to the merits under the new Massachusetts statute? Should it?

Page 1009. After note 2, add:

2.1. For a remarkable example of government contract liability, see United States v. Winstar Corp., 64 U.S.L.W. 4739 (U.S., July 1, 1996). In the 1980s, when the Federal Savings and Loan Insurance Corporation ran out of money to pay for the insured deposits of failed savings and loans, it contracted with solvent savings and loans to take over the failed ones. FSLIC contractually agreed that the solvent savings and loans could recognize the acquisition of "goodwill" in these transactions, amortize it over forty years, and count it as capital. This "capital" was illusory, but its recognition was essential to the transactions; without it, the acquiring institutions would immediately be rendered insolvent by the capital deficits of the acquired institutions. Sometime after these acquistions, Congress legislated a new rule that no federally insured savings and loan could count goodwill as capital. The acquiring institutions were immediately rendered insolvent by this amendment; some were forced to close and some succeeded in raising massive amounts of new capital.

The government argued, under several doctrinal labels, that it could not contract away its power to regulate. On the other hand, it would be hard to imagine a clearer case of actual reliance on a specific promise of particular regulatory treatment. The Court held the government liable in damages without agreeing on a majority opinion; there were two dissents. The issues debated are not really remedies issues; they are about the substantive law of government contracts. But they nicely illustrate the difficulties that are inevitable once sovereign immunity is waived.

2. Suits against Officers in Their Personal Capacities

a. Qualified Immunity

Page 1026. After note 11, add:

This holding led to a new problem: In cases where the United States is immune and the employee is not, the Attorney General may be tempted to certify that the employee was acting within the scope of his employment — whatever the facts. Thus the Attorney General certified that a federal employee in Columbia, driving drunk with an unidentified woman after midnight, was acting within the scope of his employment. Maybe so. But the Supreme Court has held that such certifications are judicially reviewable. Gutierrez de Martinez v. Lamagno, 115 S. Ct. 2227 (1995).

Page 1027. After note 12, add:

Defendants can appeal repeatedly, in different procedural contexts — once when their motion to dismiss is denied, again when their motion for summary judgment is denied. Behrens v. Pelletier, 116 S. Ct. 834 (1996).

However, denials of qualified immunity are appealable only when the appeal presents an issue of law — usually whether the relevant legal standard was clearly settled. Defendants denied immunity cannot appeal on grounds that present issues of fact or of evidentiary sufficiency. Thus, where three police officers moved for summary judgment on the ground that there was no evidence that they had beaten the plaintiff, denial of the summary judgment motion was not appealable. Johnson v. Jones, 115 S. Ct. 2151 (1995). This motion seems to go to the merits rather than the immunity, but the Court did not rely on that ground.

Page 1027. After note 2, add:

2.1. The difference in formulation has at least one consequence: A municipality's argument that it is being sued for the acts of a non-policymaking employee goes to liability and not to immunity, so an order rejecting that argument is not an appealable collateral order. Swint v. Chambers County Commission, 115 S. Ct. 1203 (1995). Compare note 12 at 1026-1027 of the main volume.

Page 1028. After note 3c, add:

3.c.i. The Court has agreed to decide another case that turns on the single act of a final policymaker. Brown v. Bryan County, 67 F.3d 1174 (5th Cir. 1995), *cert. granted as* Board of County Commissioners v. Brown, 116 S. Ct. 1540 (1996). The Bryan County sheriff, who was stipulated to be the final policymaker for the sheriff's department, knowingly hired a deputy with a long string of misdemeanors. That deputy later severely injured Mrs. Brown. The court of appeals upheld a jury verdict for plaintiff, relying on *Pembauer* to support liability against the county. The cert petition questioned whether a single act can be a policy, whether it could reflect deliberate indifference to the safety of potential plaintiffs, and whether a federal jury can override an Oklahoma statute that bars only those with felony records from serving as deputies.

b. Absolute Immunity

Page 1043. After note 12, add:

12.1. Distinguish efforts to corrupt the judicial process from the outside, at issue in *Dennis*, from "all persons—governmental or otherwise—who were integral parts of the judicial process." Briscoe v.

LaHue, 460 U.S. 325 (1983). *Briscoe* held that police officers who testify in criminal trials are absolutely immune from suit for damages caused by their alleged perjury. *Briscoe* has been extended to a wide range of judicial adjuncts, often under the label "quasi-judicial immunity." Examples include mediators, arbitrators, case evaluators, court-appointed monitoring committees, law clerks, probation officers, a psychiatrist who interviewed a criminal defendant, and law enforcement officials who execute a facially valid court order. Some of the cases are collected in Wagshal v. Foster, 28 F.3d 1249 (D.C. Cir. 1994), and in Roland v. Phillips, 19 F.3d 552 (11th Cir. 1994).

Page 1047. After note 11, add:

12. The Court has agreed to decide whether the President is immune from suit, during his time in office, for acts not in his official capacity. Jones v. Clinton, 869 F. Supp. 690 (D. Ark. 1994), *rev'd*, 72 F.3d 1354 (8th Cir.), *cert. granted*, 64 U.S.L.W. 3847 (June 26, 1996). The alleged tort occurred, if at all, before the President took office. The district judge, and the dissenting judges in the court of appeals, feared that active litigation would interfere with the President's ability to perform his office, and that a judge scheduling the President's time would violate separation of powers. Judge McMillian, dissenting from denial of rehearing en banc, 81 F.3d 78 (8th Cir. 1996), noted that President Nixon was already out of office when *Harlow* was filed. No one contends that the President cannot be sued at all for unofficial acts; the district court permitted discovery but stayed all other proceedings until the President left office. The court of appeals vacated the stay, assuming that the trial judge would defer to the necessities of the President's schedule.

D. THE RIGHT TO JURY TRIAL

Page 1058. After note 6, add:

However that messy set of questions works out, do not confuse it with a different set: Even in legal claims triable to juries, fact issues are for the jury and legal issues are for the judge. The interpretation of a legal document is generally a legal issue, even if parol evidence is admitted to explain it. Thus, the Court recently held, the interpretation of patent claims is for the judge, even in an infringement action triable to a jury. Markman v. Westview Instruments, 116 S. Ct. 1384 (1996). On this issue too, the Court looked to analogous practice in 1791.

Page 1060. After note 12, add:

Kentucky enacted a rule eliminating jury trial in cases that were too complicated for a jury to intelligently try. The state supreme court struck the rule down as a violation of the state constitutional right to jury trial. Steelvest, Inc. v. Scansteel Service Center, 908 S.W.2d 104 (Ky. 1995).